Fred Brown moved from darkest city to deepest country a few years ago and now writes from his cottage in South-East Kent.

FRED BROWN

Happy

The Life of a Working Sheepdog

GRAFTON BOOKS
A Division of the Collins Publishing Group

LONDON GLASGOW
TORONTO SYDNEY AUCKLAND

Grafton Books
A Division of the Collins Publishing Group
8 Grafton Street, London W1X 3LA

A Grafton Paperback Original 1987

ISBN 0-586-07064-8

Printed and bound in Great Britain by
Collins, Glasgow

Set in Times

For my sister SYLVIA
with love and gratitude

The calves peered both over and through the gate, probably wondering what all the commotion was about. Our entire family – wife, three daughters and self – were spread out and advancing down the next field, a picture of resolution. Before us were fifty sheep apparently as determined to frustrate us as we were to pen them.

We drove them on, occasionally needing to back track to retrieve two or three of the more bloody minded, but eventually the lot were nicely bunched near the entrance to a penned area leading to our separating gate through which as they passed, necessarily in single file, we planned to pick off the ones requiring detailed foot inspections.

With my wife and I at the extreme ends of our human chain, we all five slowly closed in. Inexplicably the sheep wouldn't budge. Normally the leaders take the rest with them. On this occasion, with half a dozen actually already inside the pen, the remainder stubbornly milled around at the entrance.

I shouted to the children to come in closer. One of them, an enthusiast in most things, shot forward, only a few strides but enough to panic the nearest sheep through a gap in the chain. This time the vanguard triggered the rest, and within seconds the entire flock was at the other end of the field. There was simply nothing else for it but to start the whole miserable business all over again.

Time after time since arriving on the farm we human sheepdogs, new to rural ways and accomplishments, had tried to round up the flock, usually achieving little more than blaming each other for the resultant confusion as the wily old sheep continued to exploit our lack of co-ordination.

Pandemonium triumphed!

Even the sheep laughed at our ineptitude. With or without the help of all unsuspecting callers at the farm roped in willy-nilly, the outcome was usually unsatisfactory if not downright calamitous. What we needed, quite simply, was a sheepdog.

Our favourite TV programme illustrated how easy it was to control sheep! A few magical words or signals, and the dog was away to work like clockwork as the sheep tamely fell into line. If any dared assert itself, harmony was quickly restored by the dog's immediate response to word or whistle from the shepherd. Beyond the slightest doubt we needed a sheepdog!

I started to make enquiries, and my neighbours were encouraging, one in particular with two superb dogs which worked cows and sheep equally well. In next to no time I picked up a tremendous amount about how to train a sheepdog, for most owners, I quickly discovered, once provided with a good listener, need no prompting to reminisce about their experience and modest expertise in selecting a puppy and training it as a partner on the farm.

The fact remained, though well briefed about what to do with my puppy sheepdog once I had it, I was no nearer actually to finding one. The farmer with two superb dogs told me I was welcome to one of his next whelps, but also warned me I'd have a long wait. He'd only just sold the last litter, and didn't intend to mate their mother when next she came into season. 'Give her a bit of a rest,' he'd said.

Feeling not only disappointed but desperate, I also enquired about buying a trained dog. But it wasn't only the price that put me off. When I thought about it, I realized how much I wanted to train my own dog. Theoretically, my ignorance being what it was, nothing could have been more misguided, yet a gut feeling persisted that the sort of working relationship I wanted stood a better chance if the puppy and I learned together.

Paradoxically, by one of those strange sequences of events that normally belong only to story books, I was led to the dog in making enquiries about a calf.

Driving through the next village I'd seen a couple of Jersey cows, and wondered what happened to their calves. I knocked on the door of the nearest farmhouse, and the man who answered eventually overcame his country caution, not to say suspicion, to admit I was really looking for the driver of a blue van. My reluctant informant either didn't know or wasn't prepared to divulge the name and address.

A few days later, driving through the same village, I spotted a blue van parked opposite a row of cottages. A knock at one door led me to two along, and soon I was talking to Bill Wheel.

In leisurely silence he took a tin from his trouser pocket, rolled himself a cigarette, repeatedly re-lit it, all the time, I was aware, sizing me up. Barely uttered a word.

I now know that Bill is the opposite of laconic. Once at ease his talk sounds like a machine gun firing monosyllables, but first you have to win his confidence, meaning merely convince him you're not out to do him down.

'Yes,' he warily admitted, 'I own the Jerseys.'

Our conversation, such as it was, lasted five minutes at most. The younger cow, daughter of the other, was to calve on the 24th of next month. He might sell it. All depended. Might keep it. Too early to say. No use rushing into these things. It was agreed I should return on the 24th or thereabouts.

When I did, on the day itself, Bill was all smiles. A lovely heifer calf, born the day before, no complications, delivered on his own. 'I think I'll keep her, she's a beauty,' he concluded.

Rolling another cigarette he told one of his Jack Russells to be quiet. 'Silly bugger,' he laughed, adding, perhaps to put me at my ease, the dog hated children. 'Can't abide 'em, not since a lad in the village came to play with my grandson, and tormented the dog almost out of its mind. Lucky it didn't bite him. Served him right if it had.'

He turned affectionately to the dog. 'Wonderful killer of foxes, wonderfully brave.' Once more he re-lit his cigarette. 'Would you believe,' he dared me not to, 'we send him underground with a transmitter on his collar, he corners the fox, but by the time we dig it out it's dead.' The dog, loving the limelight, yapped like mad.

I confessed I'd seen only one fox in my entire life, in the woods on the boundary of the farm; I pointed in the general direction. His eyes filled with disbelief. One fox! At my age!

'I paid £428 for my old van,' he suddenly introduced what I took to be a totally unrelated subject. '£428,' he again sucked on the sum, 'a lot of money even in these days.' His eyes darted from the van to me. 'Do you know how I paid for it?' He waited. Smiled. 'Foxes. Thirty-one foxes, £11 for the cheapest, £25 for the best.'

The new light in his eyes, unlike his fag, didn't go out. 'I made my own snares, the sliding type that hold the fox without strangling it. Not the other bloody sort,' he spit out his contempt, 'you know, the ones that lock tighter every time the fox struggles to get free. Chokes the poor

10

bugger in the end. 'My snares,' he admitted, 'are cruel. But the others are bloody cruel.'

With this subtle distinction teasing my mind I turned from Jack Russell's now silent belligerence to the purpose of my visit. 'The calf!' Bill reacted. 'I think I'll keep her, but I'll let you know. Really is a beauty.'

Little more than a week later I met him driving away from our village garage. He stopped and wound down the window. 'The vet,' he called, 'tells me to keep her. Too good to sell, he says.'

Bill's leather face slowly stiffened into seriousness not to say sadness. 'Trouble is, I can't really afford to keep her. Don't know what to do.'

Next day I again called at his house. 'Funny thing,' he welcomed me, 'I was just thinking of you. And my lovely calf. Greedy little blighter she is,' he laughed, 'getting on a treat.'

A week later his blue van pulled up in front of our farmhouse. Jack Russell's yapping alerted me, but Bill made no attempt to get out as I approached. Just sat looking, taking in the scene. 'So this is where you live;' he eventually unwound himself from the steering wheel, sauntered to the front of the van, hitched his trousers, and started to roll a cigarette, picture of a man in charge of time. His tobacco tin was half full of nub ends. 'I always keep 'em,' he explained, 'with the new tobacco. Stops it going dry.'

Bill lit his cigarette, spat out a stray piece of tobacco, and asked me, begging my pardon, how old I was. His reaction to my admission left me in no doubt. 'You know old Fred?' he waited for confirmation; 'how old do you think he is?'

Now everybody knew old Fred, even comparative new-comers like ourselves. He was something of a legendary

11

figure in his own lifetime. We all marvelled not only at his ceaseless activity but his ageless agility. Like a man half his years he climbed on and off his ubiquitous bike, dug drains, cut lawns, built walls, trimmed hedges, cleared gardens run wild. You name it, he did it. In fact he'd already helped us with our hedging and ditching. So in comparing my years with old Fred, Bill obviously thought we looked the same age!

Nevertheless, having made this point, he felt constrained to mention he and old Fred had more in common than their youthfulness and industry. They loved insulting each other. 'All in good fun, you understand.'

To illustrate his meaning Bill described a stranger in the village pub nervously asking the publican if they were spoiling for a fight. 'Fight!' the man behind the bar added to the confusion, 'those two are bosom friends.'

Bill could hardly speak for laughing. 'Poor chap, he didn't understand our sense of humour.'

I asked about the calf. He looked pained. 'D'you know, I told you the calf was due for weaning on the 23rd of next month! Well, I said to the wife this morning, it's this month, not next. Somehow got it mixed up.'

He waited for the unmixing to register. 'Greedy little bugger, already sucked her mother's teats sore. She'll need solids soon, something to get her teeth into apart from her mother's teats,' he chuckled.

'You mean,' the penny dropped, 'you'll have to charge extra? If you decide to sell her!'

'Did I ever tell you,' he responded, 'about my freak lamb? I saw the ewe was having trouble, pushed my hand inside, felt one head, then another, but couldn't sort out the legs. The vet came and told me I had a lamb with two heads. Had a hell of a job getting it down the birth passage. Dead, of course.'

I must have looked sceptical. 'It's the truth, I tell you.' And as though to emphasize his inability not to speak the truth he claimed his only other freak was a chicken with four legs. 'I kept it in spirits for a long time,' he offered conclusive proof.

'How much extra?' I asked.

'Not to worry,' he wound himself back into the van, 'you'll find I'm a fair-minded man.' Then, seemingly as an afterthought, he wondered whether I'd mentioned to old Fred we were looking for a sheepdog puppy?

The idea took me completely by surprise. For a start old Fred didn't own a dog, and wasn't interested. Unashamedly he was a cat man, keeping a couple at home, and half a dozen at least on his allotment. Seeing him digging one evening I'd leaned over the gate for a chat, and been introduced to the latter gang, all of them half-wild and largely self-supporting by their aptitude for killing rabbits.

'Have a word with Fred,' advised Bill, 'I think he might be able to help you.' So not wasting a moment more than necessary, that night, in fact, I went in search of Fred first to his allotment where he was just about to climb on his bike homeward bound.

'Bill mentioned you were after a dog,' he didn't waste time on formalities, 'I think I've found one for you.' And he told me a rather involved story about his brother in the next village having a drinking friend who knew a farmer whose wife had told his wife their dog, indispens-able on the farm, was whelping any time now. In fact, Fred added, she might have had 'em already. He went on to say they were bound to be good 'uns seeing both parents were working farm dogs.

I don't know how many times this point had been made by farmers and friends in the village alike. Never mind, we were told, about pedigrees as long as your arm or sheepdog trial winners no matter how famous, the first essential was to get a puppy whose parents were involved in day-to-day farm work. Even this guaranteed nothing in what was inescapably a risky business, but at least the offspring of working farm dogs offered reason for hope.

Fred told me he'd find out for sure the farmer's name and address, and let me know. Meanwhile, he said, did we want a couple of cats to keep the rats and rabbits down?

Next morning, needing to put the flock through the footrot bath, our human chain spread itself across the field and gently advanced. Progress was satisfactory. Admittedly I occasionally raised my voice to suggest one or other of us was getting too close or leaving too wide a gap, but remarkably quickly given the circumstances the sheep were penned and ready for their single-file hygienic parade.

Then one of our links, normally utterly reliable, took it into her head that the handful of sheep at the back milling round harmlessly away from the rest should be moved nearer the front. Never mind that the ones already at the front were congested at the single-file entrance to the walk-through bath, the ones at the back were driven forward causing general panic and a stampede to the other end of the pen. They jostled and fought, the ones at the rear frantically packing the rest like sardines as they struggled to defy our efforts to turn them.

Finally one of the hurdles gave, allowing the flock to pour out to the other end of the field. With one prostrate exception! Apparently suffocated in the crush, something we'd never been warned against by either our neighbours or the sheep manuals, it lay as dead.

What to do? Give it the kiss of life? I grabbed the carcass and propped it up between my legs, but immediately support was withdrawn it collapsed, rolling on its side. I tried again, this time shaking it, though what I hoped this would achieve I can't now imagine. The fact remains, when it once more fell in a heap, it started to kick as if in some sort of convulsion, and eventually opened its eyes.

Yet again I heaved it to its feet, did a bit more shaking, and hoped. The transformation was almost unbelievable. The sheep shook itself like a dog after a bath, started to struggle with growing determination, and shot off to join the others apparently none the worse for the experience.

We'd just managed to get the flock back into the pen with the first sheep moving through the footrot bath when Fred cycled up. He handed me a phone number. 'I've had a word with my brother,' he said; 'you'd better give the farmer a ring. Don't hang about, there'll be more buyers than puppies.'

So while I finished the sheep my wife arranged a visit to the place of sale, encouraged by the farmer's confidence he'd have just what we needed.

We were greeted by both the man and his wife, she leading us to the barn, he singing the praises of the puppies' parents; the father, top dog on the farm, sired superb whelps, lots of them already indispensable on farms throughout the county, the mother, slightly younger, worked the flock like a champion. This latest litter of seven was well up to standard, and seeing we wanted a dog to help us on our farm we should have first choice.

As soon as the barn door was opened we found ourselves surrounded by puppies, tumbling over each other in their anxiety to be first. The children laughingly each picked up two, leaving one, we then noticed, sitting in isolation. It licked my wife's hand, tried to bite it, licked a bit more, all the time wagging its tail. She looked at me, I looked at the children. To make a choice was impossible.

Adding to my uncertainty were a couple of books by men with international reputations for both breeding and training sheepdogs. Naturally I'd read them assiduously, aware of my almost total ignorance. One said ignore the puppy that makes no attempt to rush toward you and sits on its own; the other that such behaviour was not in itself evidence of inferiority, indeed, that this tendency might well indicate an introspective dog, one capable of reflection and above-average thoughtfulness in tackling working dilemmas. The experts were, however, utterly agreed about one thing. As far as selecting a puppy for training as a farm dog was concerned, everything, not least the final outcome, was in the lap of the gods. The best we could hope for was an inspired guess.

The children could hardly have disagreed more! Concerned about little but appearances, not beauty but indefinable appeal tugging at the heart strings, their choice was the one with, they insisted, the cheekiest look. From this standpoint it seemed indistinguishable from the rest, but they were adamant. The one on its own, still playfully licking and biting and wagging, won their nomination.

To be honest, I had my doubts. Allowing for the uncertainty of selection, agreed by the experts, I couldn't forget the man whose vast experience made him so confident that isolationist puppies were to be avoided. At all cost! We couldn't afford to make a mistake.

Remembering a bit of *unanimous* advice from the experts, I asked the children to put the puppies down, and sharply clapped my hands. A couple scarpered to the far end of the barn, obviously unsure, two started to go with them but looked back half way, the rest conspicuously ignored the noise altogether; they were either deaf or brave. One of them, I noticed, was the children's choice.

Even so, it looked smaller than the others, not skinny or remotely a weakling, but still rather tiny. And staring at it hard, I realized that what the children called a cheeky face struck me as more pathetic. Was this, I wondered, the true nature of its appeal to them?

Recalling an old countryman's advice that a well bred pup should weigh heavily when handled, I picked it up; beyond doubt in this case looks were deceptive.

The farmer and his wife laughed at our indecision. 'They're all good 'uns,' he said, 'specially that one,' he pointed to the biggest. 'But we want a bitch,' my wife whispered, clearly on the children's side. In the end we never did make a deliberate choice, at least I didn't. It was simply assumed we were having the puppy fussed over by the children or rather fussed over most. All that remained was to convince them to leave it at the farm for another fortnight or so until it was weaned.

In this period another incident, this time unrelated to the sheep, supposedly underlined the urgency of our need of a dog. Roaming the farmyard, definitely appealing to our romantic ideas of country living, were our free-range hens and a magnificent cockerel. Actually, though I say roaming, the cockerel never did less than strut like a self-appointed king of all he surveyed including the children's freedom to move unmolested about the farm.

First intimation he was turning really nasty was when my wife as usual shortly before lunch went to collect the eggs. Normally he ignored her, but this time he danced

17

menacingly in her path, pawed the ground like a bull spoiling for a fight, and finally flew at her face. She returned to the farmhouse white and shaken, not so much afraid as startled.

We now have every reason to know that cockerels can be not only aggressive but vicious with it. The time wasn't far distant when drastic and dreaded action would be required, but until this first attack we blithely assumed he felt about us as we about him. And our disillusionment was speedily reinforced. That afternoon one of the twins rushed in from school to say her sisters were trapped in the farmyard, their only way of escape cut off by the strutting marauder.

I was still feeling sceptical as I stepped out to investigate. It didn't seem possible that our erstwhile pride and joy should be capable of such antagonism, playfully menacing maybe, but not this downright warfare. As soon as he saw me he ceased patrolling outside the barn where the children had taken refuge, and made a beeline, clearly looking for trouble and refusing not to find it.

Indignantly I lashed out with my wellington boots. For a second he fluttered back before flying for my face, and persisted as I fought him off with arms and legs. Incredible. Our lovely cockerel! I grabbed a stick and chased him right out of the farmyard. But next morning at egg-collecting time he was just as bad.

'The dog will see him off,' my wife laughed, and I shared the joke – until I saw she actually meant it, never more serious. To leave me in no doubt she added: 'The dog won't stand any nonsense.'

Hang on a moment. I reminded her the dog would be about eight weeks old when we brought her home, and wouldn't be trained for months. Meanwhile, dog or no dog, she'd better carry a stout stick when she collected the eggs.

'We'll see,' she smiled.

A fortnight or so later, answering a phone call, we returned to the farm to collect the puppy. As before her brothers and sisters rushed to greet us. She alone stayed behind, apparently not interested, barely even looking in our direction. Doubt overwhelmed me. Perhaps after all we'd made a terrible mistake.

'My Bess,' the farmer nodded toward the loner, 'was like that as a whelp; rarely bothered with the rest of the litter. One of my best dogs now. You can't tell at this stage how they'll turn out.'

Like a drowning man clutching at straws I held on to that, but in any case my renewed doubts were swept aside as the children blissfully fought off the other puppies to gather up the object of their choice and argue as to whose turn it was to hold her.

Excitedly one of them carried her to the car while the other two, heeding the farmer's advice, collected an armful of the litter's bedding, persuaded by him that the scent of the mother and the other whelps would reassure our puppy as it settled in new surroundings. We pushed the bedding into the boot, and with the children still arguing about whose turn it was next to do the cuddling and for how long made our way home.

From the start we chose to keep the puppy in the kitchen of the farmhouse. Some farmers won't allow their dogs inside the house. They believe a working dog as distinct from a domestic pet is better off in a kennel or a corner of the barn. To allow it indoors, they argue, gives it a false impression, makes it soft and therefore unsuitable for the rough and tumble of life on a farm.

Right or wrong – and I still believe they're sincerely mistaken – our sheepdog puppy was introduced to a snug basket not far from our Rayburn stove.

Two practical matters immediately confronted us – house training and – infinitely more important as far as the children were concerned – a name. Understandably, the name tantalized us all almost from the moment the puppy was finally chosen. During the fortnight's wait we discussed it as a family on numerous occasions, but found agreement less than straightforward.

The children favoured what I thought of as conventional names like Rover and Bruno, perfectly acceptable in an urban setting, but for a working sheepdog somehow inappropriate.

Funny thing about naming farm animals, cow, pig, goat, dog or whatever. Without a name the animal is largely anonymous, one of a group with little to distinguish it or at least make it distinctive. But once named it takes on a character or personality which adds a new dimension of dignity and changes the nature of all subsequent relationships. This, in any case, was our experience.

As the sheep and the two housecows and the two pigs arrived we named each of them with care. When the flock grew too big to make this impracticable, though we still knew the sheep individually and were able to identify them readily, it wasn't quite the same. A name represents intimacy and endearment.

No wonder we agonized over a name for the puppy. And at the end of the day she herself chose it for us. Six years later anything but Happy seems out of the question.

Hearing of our decision an old shepherd told me

working dogs are better off with a one syllable name; easier and quicker for them to understand from a distance. 'What's wrong with Floss or Shep?' he asked. I saw his point, and thought we might have made a mistake, but experience since gives us no reason to regret our decision. In fact, any other name is, as I say, unthinkable.

Next came the house training. When I was a lad the only dog we ever had, a mongrel answering to the inappropriate name of Sparky, was encouraged what not to do by the method then prevalent – his nose was rubbed in the result of his other end's indiscipline. I believed this to be misguided then, and am even more against the practice now.

Our puppy already knew, taught by its mother, not to foul its bedding. No intelligent dog is going to allow her whelps to make any sort of mess that detracts from her own and their comfort, the assumption being, of course, that the puppies are able to relieve themselves elsewhere. If the sides of the basket or box are too high, little wonder the bedding quickly resembles a compost heap!

Happy's basket, sides high enough to prevent draughts, provided an easy exit. Yes, but to where? Little use transferring the mess from the bedding to the kitchen floor or the lounge carpet. What was required was a place for emergencies indoors where Happy the puppy could relieve herself with little inconvenience to anyone, and even more important have regular opportunities to do the needful outside.

We already had a catflap, and immediately began to train her to use it simply by pushing her through each time she went out and returned, but meanwhile an old newspaper near her basket was provided for unavoidable emergencies, careful watch being taken initially to ensure she associated the two. Inevitably we had the usual

21

mistakes, but in less time than we dared hope she cottoned on to what was required, primarily, I'm sure, because she was given ample chance to get out of doors.

This early intensive training placed upon us a serious obligation, for soon Happy was incapable of relieving herself anywhere but on grass. And the discomfort if she couldn't get out, an easy oversight as she outgrew the catflap, made us extra careful. Actually, living where we did, the kitchen door was left open virtually permanently even at night. By the time winter made this impossible Happy knew what was required last thing at night and availed herself of regular opportunities during the day.

Her training for farm work, treated by both of us at first as more of a game than training, started when she was four months, thought rather young by some experts but not by Happy herself. She was already answering to her name and came when called. Likewise she quickly picked up when she wasn't wanted. As I left the farmhouse I sometimes found she was bounding after me. The first half dozen times or so I sent her back; and I mean *sent* – she responded to my voice and arm pointing in the direction of the farmhouse.

But this playful persistence on her part persuaded me one morning to allow her to accompany me to the far side of the farm where I was repairing fences, a story of my life, and to my surprise she wasn't any trouble. On the contrary her company added to my enjoyment or more correctly helped to relieve the monotony. Most days after that she joined me on routine chores, never, however, if I was handling the cows, sheep or goats.

The last thing I wanted was for one of our older ewes or worse still rams butting her into fear of the animals generally, but fortunately she showed little interest; a casual glance occasionally in their direction, but not the slightest sign she wanted to chase them. The same could not be said for her attitude to the ducks and hens, though whether they appreciated her idea of fun is open to question.

I came across her in the farmyard *eyeing* first of all the ducks. They'd just been fed and were waddling their leisurely way back to the pond at the back of the old barn. Happy didn't so much herd them as follow them, but I couldn't fail to notice how concentrated was her stare. Crouched low and creeping forward she fixed her eyes on the ducks which weren't even aware of her presence until, patience exhausted, she suddenly sent them squawking.

Not surprisingly sheepdogs herd instinctively, and a good job too, otherwise they'd be little use for farm work. However, if this instinct lacks breeding and refinement it turns the dog into a predator, a killer; if ever you've seen a sheep savaged by a rogue dog you'll know what I mean.

Now one of the ways this herding instinct expresses itself is by how the dog eyes the sheep, which explains why some sheepdogs are referred to as strong-eyed, normally a compliment but if excessive a liability. Certainly they need to eye the sheep, watch them like a hawk if they're to remain in control, but some sheepdogs are so strong-eyed they become transfixed or stupefied, and don't even snap out of it when the shepherd's commands become heated.

On the other hand, a dog without this essential quality is hopeless, incapable of being trained, and possibly a coward too. All the patience in the world won't turn it into a working partner.

Happy eyed the ducks or hens at every opportunity, following their every move, initially keeping her distance, but finally she was defeated by her own playfulness or impetuosity. For all that, I felt reassured that her early idea of fun was to herd. First the ducks; then the hens; then – her waterloo.

In the event I suspect she wasn't herding at all, merely playing round the feet of one of our housecows, something I shouldn't have allowed at this stage. But before either of us knew what was happening she hit the dust or more accurately the mud, helped on her way by a provoked hoof.

Straightaway I could see she'd come to no harm, but this didn't entirely silence my fears. A shepherd of long experience, chatting with me about training sheepdogs, warned me that the most intelligent dog sometimes associated an unpleasant incident with anyone who happened to be present at the time. 'The dog's not to know,' he said. 'If you're there the animal will think you're somehow responsible.'

I remembered how he went on about this as he illustrated how too many owners either praised or corrected their dog belatedly. No use, he grumbled, expecting the dog to understand the treatment being handed out was for something that happened five or even two minutes ago. Its only concern was what was happening now, meaning that pleasure or pain, like praise or punishment, was related to the last occurrence. Makes me wild, he told me, the way some people punish their dog the first time they see it or catch it often long after the offence. 'I've known dogs to run off, and be punished for coming home,' his eyes blazed, 'at least that's how the dog must have seen it.'

I just hoped Happy didn't associate me with the pain of the housecow's hoofing, and felt reassured as immediately she rushed toward me for comfort and protection.

At the same time I hoped she'd learned enough from the experience to be wary the next time.

Judging by the way she followed me for the rest of the morning, all was well. Indeed, she didn't altogether stop *eyeing* the same housecow, but from the kind of distance you'd expect an intelligent puppy to observe.

During these early weeks and months, the cow episode apart, Happy's life was virtually carefree. What training we did I tried to make fun, certainly more fun than work.

I began by encouraging her to lie down, gently pushing her low and keeping her in that position. My only concern was to imprint the *sound* of my voice with what I wanted; it wouldn't have mattered to Happy if in teaching her to lie down I'd used the words stand up or roll over, so long as the sound was consistent with the stance I wished her to adopt.

Before our need of a sheepdog compelled me seriously to contemplate the training of our own, I attributed to canine intelligence the ability to understand human language. My mother claimed that our mongrel of long ago could understand her every word, and this common misapprehension stuck in my mind.

Now, however, I knew the sound not the language was what mattered, evidenced by the way some shepherds communicate with their dog by simply varying the tone of their whistle. Makes not a scrap of difference to the dog's understanding.

Happy was quick on the uptake but too much like a coiled spring as she tried to please me by lying down and staying down in the same place. She'd manage it for a few seconds before exploding toward me, tail wagging, eyes dancing, no less irrepressible as irresistible. Patiently we tried again. And again. Within a month she was lying down to command, and staying there as I backed away before calling her for a generous helping of praise. So far so good.

Incidentally, I found that praise was a far better teacher than punishment. This is not to say I didn't sometimes find it necessary to tap Happy on the nose or give her a good shaking to indicate my disapproval, but beyond doubt praise at the slightest justification proved much more instructive, not least because she was so keen to please.

I mustn't give the impression that training at this stage occupied much of our time. We spent a good deal of every day simply enjoying each other's company as I continued with the dreaded hedging and ditching, and otherwise worked in different parts of the farm. Happy showed little inclination to stray too far. If ever she was out of sight I called and invariably she bounded toward me without hesitation.

Strangely enough, to my great good fortune, I never from the start had much difficulty from this standpoint. She came when I called, not always instantaneously, of course, particularly at first, but come she did without overmuch shouting.

Significantly she still showed little real interest in the sheep, a casual glance occasionally, but nothing like her aptitude for eyeing the hens and ducks. Happy found the waddlers and strutters irresistible and often made their lives less than peaceful. Crouching low, creeping forward, her eyes riveted, she finally sent them literally flying. But never the cockerel. How she knew to give him a wide berth I can only attribute to her intelligence. His reign of terror continued, and wouldn't have stopped, I'm sure, at the approach of the dog. Something would have to be done about his fierce independence, but exactly what we weren't sure. All other considerations apart, we actually liked him. On second thoughts, perhaps *liked* is too strong, specially when his belligerence extended to the children, but beyond doubt we admired his magnificence. And the way he greeted first light appealed to our romantic expectations of country life.

As for the rest of the farm animals I took good care to keep Happy away from them particularly after her encounter with the hoof. She was still only seven months, and the last thing I wanted was to have her confidence undermined. The kick from the cow appeared to have done no harm at all, but only the foolhardy would have exposed her to the possibility of similar experiences.

I remembered an old farmer full of wisdom telling me that few things hindered the development of a sheepdog more than a premature confrontation with the sheep and most of all a ram or bullock. 'Makes 'em a bag of nerves,' he said. 'Sheepdogs are brave and strong, given time. Don't rush 'em. They'll tell you when they're ready to work.'

How often I thought of his advice as our chain of human sheepdogs continued inadequately to deputize; and sometimes, taken unawares, I was the only sheepdog available!

The first time this happened the phone rang and a voice said did I know some of our sheep were on the road leading to the next village? Impossible. Not more than an hour before I'd checked them, grazing as contented as could be on the far side of the farm. Admittedly the fencing there was suspect, necessitating makeshift repairs the week before, but nothing like bad enough to permit a break-out.

'You'd better get over here a bit sharpish,' the village policeman sounded less than his genial self.

Now there's one good thing I can say about straying sheep. Once they've turned homeward they retrace their steps to the same gap in the fence and usually scurry through without too much bother. Yes, but first I had to turn them on my own which involved getting them together from various points alongside the road and driving them through a narrow gateway. The policeman was sympathetic but not inclined to get his boots muddy.

To top it all, passing motorists appeared to see only the funny side of my problems. The presence of the police car made them circumspect, but not to the extent of stopping them laughing their heads off as the sheep darted in all directions but through that bloody gate. If ever my exasperation, never mind my embarrassment, felt the need of a sheepdog it was then.

I ran this way and that, desperate to get the sheep off the road, but frustrated time and again by their reluctance to pass through the gateway. Eventually one of them ventured, and the rest followed, all seven of them immediately breaking into a trot across first a ploughed field and then another of young winter wheat on the boundary of our farm.

Feeling almost sanguine, I strolled behind watching them find their way home, until somebody in the adjacent wood fired a shot. A horde of wood pigeons took off, pheasants squawked, and the sheep veered to the left, dead in line for a neighbouring farmer's flock. In no time they were swallowed in the crowd; and I knew I had big problems. Seven sheep among two hundred!

Remarkably the farmer didn't stop smiling as I told him of my dilemma. 'Not to worry,' he called to his two dogs, 'we might as well do the job now before it gets dark.' So the four of us, two walking to heel, made our way to his flock.

28

He snapped out a couple of commands, the dogs raced away to approach from opposite sides, and painlessly the sheep moved toward a separating race. Within twenty minutes or so of my knocking on his door, my seven were picked off, his two hundred were back where they belonged, and I was free to continue my journey home, aided part way by his dogs. I'd heard of helpful neighbours but this was something else.

No further mishaps, and the welcome I received from Happy took on a new meaning. One day soon, I ruminated, such nightmares will belong to the past! In fact, this experience, apart from encouraging me to push on with repairs to the fencing, added I see in retrospect an element of urgency to our training programme, something I was trying to avoid.

What I wasn't trying to avoid was to pick the brains of Bill Wheel. The more I got to know him the more I appreciated his remarkable knowledge of country life, wild animals no less than farm stock, and his initial cautiousness swung to the other extreme as he took me under his wing. Not that we met often, we were both too busy, but occasionally he called to tell me he'd heard of a good calf for sale, and once for no other reason than to give me an invitation.

I saw his blue van approaching long before it arrived, and was waiting in the farmyard as characteristically he took his time to unwind his long legs from behind the steering wheel. 'Want the chance to see some foxes?' He took out his tobacco tin and started to roll himself a cigarette. For a moment I thought he was pulling my leg, harping back to my admission I'd seen only one, something about which he'd teased me on a few occasions already, but ignoring my silence he said a shepherd friend of his was having trouble with foxes, and planned a night hunt.

A phone call to confirm the arrangements came about three days later. The shepherd and Bill were going within the hour. I was welcome to join them.

We climbed out of the van in the depth of the country about five miles away, and immediately conversation became sparse. Bill carried a torch, the shepherd a gun. Over a hedge the beam pierced the darkness round a field picking out numerous pairs of eyes. Rabbits. Then it stopped.

'A fox,' whispered Bill. It stared into the light, apparently more puzzled than fearful, making not the slightest attempt to escape the glare. The distance was the whole width of the field.

Raising the back of his hand to his mouth, Bill began to imitate, as he put it, a rabbit in distress. He'd mentioned this to me some time before, but to be honest my scepticism hadn't been entirely overcome. Now I watched as the fox moved toward us still seemingly indifferent to the beam fixed directly on it.

'Thinks it's on to an easy supper,' the shepherd explained barely audibly as the fox, at first cautious, suddenly quickened to make straight for us. And there it stood, not more than twenty strides away, its suspicions battling with its appetite.

Hardly daring to breathe I watched awestruck. The fox looked magnificent, anything but a cunning killer of newborn lambs. Bill maintained his imitation squeaking and kept the fox in the centre of the beam. It seemed glued to the spot, clearly cagey but held by the imaginary rabbit's distress.

The shepherd took aim. I gritted my teeth, too identified with the fox to watch yet too intrigued not to. The wait became excruciating. Slowly the shepherd lowered his gun. 'The hedge is too high to get it in my sights,' he murmured, adding almost apologetically: 'I hate shooting foxes.'

Bill removed the back of his hand from his mouth, and the fox, having lingered to be sure an easy kill wasn't on, nonchalantly turned away, totally unaware of its lucky escape.

Moving up the field the light picked out two rabbits; in seconds they were dispatched and slung round the waist of the shepherd who first wrung their necks, just to be sure. 'Poor little buggers,' he muttered.

Within ten minutes we sighted our second fox, far on the other side of the adjacent field, its eyes as distinctive as diamonds under a spotlight. And once more the imitation squeaking proved irresistible. The fox ran across the top of the field, followed the hedge toward us, hesitated as it drew nearer, but finally came on at speed to within no more than a dozen strides.

As before it made not the slightest attempt to escape the beam, staring into it as though mesmerized, an easy target for a crack shot.

'You've had your last lamb,' the shepherd dragged it into the hedge to be picked up as we returned. I gathered, by the way, he expected to sell the pelt for about £12, enough, he explained, to keep him in cartridges.

At a tree in the next field the beam picked out a crow which immediately took off into the darkness. One shot was enough. Both men were jubilant, Bill muttering curses as he flung the corpse into the ditch, and the shepherd quietly telling me that anyone who had seen a lamb with its eyes pecked out by a crow would detest the bloody bird.

Their vehemence extended to the magpie whose

wanton destructiveness amounted to vandalism. The man who hated shooting foxes laughed as his shot left fragments of the bird splattered in a tree.

Unlike the crow and magpie, the next victim, a wood pigeon, made no attempt to leave its roost, and fell like a stone. Nevertheless, to be sure it was dead, Bill stuck the top of its head between his teeth and bit hard, a common practice in the country, he claimed, despite the shepherd's obvious revulsion.

Never mind the recent sound of the gun, another fox responded almost immediately to the imitation squeaking, hurrying down the side of the next field, and becoming cautious only as it neared the light. The squeaking intensified. The fox crept closer, not sure or perhaps puzzled by the conspicuous absence of an audible rabbit.

Still it came on, occasionally dodging back a few strides before retracing its steps, captivated by the sound, totally ignoring the beam which provided a perfect view for us.

The shepherd kept his gun by his side, proof of how much he hated shooting foxes; and watching this one parading its every attractive feature for our pleasure, I could readily understand why.

The only noise came from Bill still sucking on the back of his hand, tantalizing the fox which incredibly remained totally indifferent to our presence. Then suddenly, perhaps picking up our scent, it fled though periodically stopping to stare into the light.

We collected the dead fox, dispatched three more rabbits, and – almost back at our starting point – casually swung the beam over the next field. The eyes of a fox stood out on the far side, and once more the simulated squeaking brought it on apace.

Reminded of his lambs, the shepherd took aim, but was diverted this time not by his hatred of shooting foxes but another fox approaching from an angle of ninety degrees, unnoticed until it was almost on top of us. Both were apparently too single-minded about the prospect of an easy kill to be aware of each other. They looked into the light, hardly moving at all, captivated by the noisy invisible rabbit.

The shepherd raised his gun. Bang. The fox dropped like a log. Bang. The second fox leaped in the air and fell dead. Bill whooped with delight. The shepherd appeared saddened by his own deadly shooting.

Three foxes in less than two hours, five sighted! 'Nothing unusual,' Bill sounded expansive, 'it's only a question of knowing where to look.'

I couldn't help but remember this the very next afternoon when Happy and I came across old Fred on the side of the farm near the woods. He was looking around nervously, obviously searching for something.

'Have you,' he appeared apologetic, 'have you come across a cat? My tom.'

It was hard to disappoint him, and I also wondered aloud whether even his half-wild tom would wander so far from the allotment. His pitying reaction clearly showed how little I knew about his beloved cats.

'Can't understand it,' he struggled for words. 'Never disappears for more than a day. Never. I haven't seen him for a week. Hope nothing's happened to him. I've looked everywhere.'

Perhaps he saw my surprise, at such inconsolable concern about a half-wild tom. 'You get attached to them,' he whispered; and moved off to continue the search.

I watched him, alive to every movement, disappear into the woods, and wondered about his rugged gentleness. Old Fred, tough as nails, outdoor worker in all weathers, not above a bit of poaching with the dreaded snare so despised by unsentimental Bill Wheel, reduced almost to tears by the disappearance of his tom which stank to high heaven.

I confess I felt profoundly moved, yet at the same time, recalling something he'd told me the week before, unable not to smile at another side of his character.

'Did you know,' his incredulity rightly assumed I didn't, 'cats can count?' He waited for the bombshell to register. 'That's right, I tell you. They can count. At least up to five.'

Apparently, one of his own cats had recently had kittens in the quiet corner of a workshop some distance from the allotment. It worried him silly until he'd tracked her down.

Then, having produced her five kittens, she'd carried them one by one to her corner in the allotment shed.

'She must have counted them before she started,' he exclaimed, 'and checked in number five before she finished.'

Suitably impressed I wondered whether she might have carried the first and simply returned for the others one at a time until the place of birth was empty. His eyes pitied me.

'Cats aren't stupid,' he said, 'they can count. She saw she had five kittens, didn't go back for number six. That's what amazes me.'

Happy was dancing excitedly at my feet. I tickled her behind the ears and hoped that, come what may, I continued to feel about her as Fred felt about his cats.

Happy was already doing four things encouragingly well; not perfectly by any means, but with sufficient consistency to indicate real progress. She crouched low when I told her to lie down; stayed in that position until given permission to move; came to me when I called; and walked to heel with surprisingly little prompting. Almost from the first she seemed to realize that walking to heel was where she belonged. Of all the things she picked up quickly this gave both of us the least trouble, even less than coming when she was called. Judging by the difficulty some farmers, never mind domestic pet owners, have in trying to stop their dogs under training pulling on a lead, I was, I realized, exceptionally fortunate.

Not so, however, with teaching her to stay *standing*. No problem lying down, but to stand perfectly still with concentration for any length of time Happy found most difficult. Perhaps it was nothing more than puppy mischievousness, or more probably my lack of training experience, but time after time the spring at the centre of her personality brought her bounding in my direction, indifferent to my obvious disapproval. I was glad she came so willingly. Otherwise I sometimes despaired of her ever learning this essential requirement in a sheepdog.

For all that, I couldn't remain discouraged for long, specially after a development I'd looked for, but didn't expect to happen so soon. I've mentioned I kept Happy away from the bullocks and other farm animals likely to be too formidable for her at this tender stage. The hoofing by the housecow had scared me, not only because of possible physical damage to the dog but the more permanent damage it might have done to her enthusiasm for farm work.

So anywhere in the region of the cows and rams I simply picked her up. I wasn't concerned about the sheep so much; the vast majority showed due respect as we passed, nervously watching the dog or running in the opposite direction, while Happy herself largely ignored them.

Then one morning we were walking to a small spinney at the middle of the farm to unblock a ditch, a job already too long delayed by the pressure of other work. The sheep grazed contentedly, apart from three or four nearest to us. They saw the dog and started to run. This set the others off, and in no time the entire flock was charging to the top end of the field.

Suddenly Happy took off after them. I shouted to her repeatedly to lie down, but she was clearly too preoccupied either to hear or obey. And the harder she ran the more the sheep panicked. For a minute or so there was pandemonium, Happy like the sheep running to no purpose.

She hurled herself at the ones nearest to her, and when they swerved took up with the stragglers. Not only this, but she nipped a few on the backside, and sometimes hung on as the now frantic sheep sought to escape.

Now I appreciate you'll find this hard to believe, but coupled to my disappointment at her disobedience was my pleasure or pride, call it what you will. For here was clear evidence that we had a dog with a real interest in sheep. Make no mistake, not all members of the breed are so endowed. They might be called sheepdogs, but some of them show not the slightest interest in sheep, and without this basic requirement all the training in the world is futile.

Happy didn't yet know the difference between running the sheep and running after them, a difference as wide as the world, but she wanted to run, and this meant that training would work the transformation. So if I felt a mixture of anger and pleasure I have to confess that pleasure was easily uppermost.

36

Eventually Happy responded to my command to lie down, and, looking decidedly pleased with herself, promptly came when I called. To be honest, this placed me in another quandary. I was pleased with her for her interest in the sheep yet didn't want my praise to reinforce her running after them for the sheer hell of it. In the end, right or wrong, my delight transcended any disapproval. Never mind the ditch that needed unblocking, I nipped back to the farmhouse for mid-morning coffee and – incidentally! – to tell my wife we had a dog and a half, one destined to be the fulfilment of our highest hopes.

On the excited rebound I decided to start the next stage of Happy's training that very afternoon. For this, a traditional method I'd heard and read a lot about, we needed a pen some six strides diameter and a few ducks on the inside. I planned four, but the fourth, to say no more, refused to co-operate. So my three ducks waddled their dignified way round the pen, doubtless wondering what in the world was going on.

My aim naturally was to teach Happy to herd them without stress, quietly moving them in a clockwise or anti-clockwise direction by command. Bill Wheel swore by the method. In fact, he'd taken me to watch his brother, well known in these parts for his sheepdog training, using it with a dog the same age as Happy, almost eight months. I'd been very impressed, and picked up lots of tips, but seeing an expert operating and then facing virtually the same situation myself was another matter.

Happy's approach was too direct, not semi-circular but almost a straight line. The ducks squawked their protest at the dog's impetuosity, and didn't hang about in getting as far away as possible. On this occasion Happy didn't learn quickly. Indeed, at one stage I began to wonder whether I needed to modify my ideas about her intelligence. I know now that a dog's desirable enthusiasm requires the wisdom of long experience to handle effectively. Any trainer will tell you that a dog without enthusiasm is useless, as useless as a dog whose enthusiasm is undisciplined. There was no doubting Happy's enthusiasm, only my ability to channel it correctly.

My command for her approach from the right was *Away to me*, and she didn't need telling twice, but time and again she went almost straight to the ducks, herding them to the left truly enough, but not to their pleasure or mine. It was little consolation at the time to be told by Bill Wheel that the fault was common and easily remedied.

What distinctly helped was when I started to wave my shepherd's crook to encourage Happy to come in wide, at first on a full semi-circle, and then slightly more acutely as she picked up the idea. Nevertheless, her performance was inconsistent, for ages. Three or four times she'd make a perfect approach, and have the ducks gently waddling like country gentlemen out for a morning stroll, but the next time her impatience took her too close and too direct. Sometimes a whole session would be almost perfect, to be followed the next day by another almost the opposite.

Strangely enough her approach from the left to the command *Come bye* was more promising from the onset. Admittedly all the previous training from the right must have helped her general understanding and discipline. At any event before the end of our first session with the left-hand approach, the ducks were gently ambling to the right, not a squawk between them.

The children were impressed with Happy, but not with

me for using the ducks. I explained that this was a customary way of training sheepdogs, that far from anything cruel happening to the ducks they were barely discomforted, and in any case a well trained sheepdog was for the benefit of all the animals on the farm, not just the sheep. How often, I asked, had they seen Happy playfully scare the living daylights out of the ducks and hens? But what happened now? If she still eyed them, she never chased them. Never. And already even the cockerel was less inclined to belligerence with Happy about the farmyard. Surely they'd noticed!

They had. But remained sceptical. 'How would you like being put in a pen and chased one way then the other?' they asked. My only answer was to demonstrate how gently Happy now persuaded the ducks to move to right or left, approaching them from a nice angle and keeping her distance. Talking of the dog *demonstrating* her skills, perhaps this was why she had so much trouble in learning the right-hand approach, for when we started I allowed the children to watch much too near, providing an unfair distraction for the dog. Once more it was Bill who put me wise, this time to the importance of the dog being trained in a situation utterly free of anything likely to divert her interest and concentration. On the other hand, I think I might be looking for excuses. Either way, the fact remains that Happy's approach from the right never was as reliable as her approach from the left. Ah, well, even superb dogs are allowed their idiosyncrasies!

The time had come, I decided, for Happy to be introduced to the sheep on a working basis. She was now nine months, strong, brave, keen, responsive to my commands, and with an obvious interest in the flock. The seven commands I taught her were:

Lie down – crouch low
Stay – stand perfectly still
Here – come to me
Away to me – approach anti-clockwise
Come bye – approach clockwise
Walk on – push the flock forward
Steady – to curb enthusiasm

Her general ability at this stage was, shall we say, encouraging, most of the time. What remained was to find out how she related to the sheep in a working situation under my control. I say 'my' control, but if of course she had been trained aright it should have been possible for any experienced shepherd to work her. Actually, my wife, hardly experienced, had already tried her hand, and been both surprised and gratified at the manner of Happy's response.

The dependable Bill Wheel advised me to use, NOT, as I'd supposed, half-a-dozen tegs (young sheep which hadn't yet lambed), but docile ewes accustomed, he explained, to being worked by a dog. Avoid any awkward buggers, he laughed, we don't want the sheep chasing the dog.

Happy showed a lot of interest as we picked off and herded the six to an enclosed orchard, ideal in size for my purpose, and also sufficiently isolated to free us both from distractions. I placed a hurdle back in position at the entrance, and told Happy to lie down. She looked at me expectantly, apparently aware the occasion was special. As for the ewes they were clearly wary of the dog, but in no way agitated. At the command *Away to me* Happy made a beautifully wide approach and, not for a moment taking her eyes off the sheep, gently pushed them toward me. Maintaining her distance she kept them moving as the sheep, nicely bunched and without the slightest panic, trotted ahead, almost strolled. They hesitated only as they neared me. I shouted to Happy to stay, then to walk on. *Steady,* I called. No problems. And the sheep were where I wanted them. Happy stood perfectly still, as though she'd been working all her life. I couldn't have wished for a more encouraging start.

We began again. This time, Happy once more at my feet, I commanded *Come bye*, and she made another semi-circular approach, collected the sheep, and brought them on, barely needing any prompting from me. It was exciting to watch her work. I felt elated, almost cocky, which might explain what happened next.

As the sheep neared me I moved away to my right. Happy, not a word from me, immediately moved to her right to push them to my new position; and each time I moved she reacted accordingly, all the time keeping the sheep facing me at a suitable distance. Beside myself at this almost clockwork control, I stepped too near the sheep, startled the leading couple which bolted taking the others with them.

Happy was after them in a flash, again not waiting for any command, and as though to teach them a lesson nipped the backside of the first she reached, and hung on to the second. Her aggression was unabated. The sheep scattered, and she hurled herself at first one then another, uncharacteristically barking like crazy between the nipping and hanging on. Chaos replaced control.

My heated commands were, of course, a waste of time. If she heard them at all, in her preoccupation she made not the least attempt to obey. Eventually some sort of order was restored. The sheep milled around in the far corner of the orchard, not taking their eyes off the dog for a moment. As for Happy, she lay at my feet, breathing

41

heavily, tongue elongated, tail wagging in expectation of my usual indulgence.

Quite honestly, I was flummoxed. I didn't mind the nipping so much, knowing, as I've implied before, that tough old ewes sometimes needed a little encouragement to help them on their way, but unless this aggression was curbed, brought under strict control, I saw as clear as day that Happy was going to be as much a liability as a help.

Yes, but what to do? The last thing I wanted was to undermine her boldness, essential in a sheepdog. Somehow I needed to correct her without blunting the edge of either her courage or determination. In any case, she deserved praise for all her excellent work before I scattered the sheep, yet if I gave it to her now she would associate it with the behaviour requiring correction.

In the event I chickened out, giving to her neither praise nor correction. And walking to the farmyard feeling thoroughly at cross purposes with myself and the dog, I was grateful to see a blue van winding its way along our pitted farm track. All three of us arrived at about the same time, and typically Bill unwound himself leisurely before digging in his pocket for a tin and starting to roll himself a cigarette.

I told him about the nipping and hanging on. His weather beaten face creased into a smile. 'Not to worry,' he re-lit his cigarette, 'you need a dog that ain't afraid to tackle some of the silly buggers. A nip won't do 'em any harm.'

In my bones I felt he was wrong, but couldn't doubt the authority of his vast experience. A countryman to his finger tips he'd been working with sheep all his life; what he didn't know about them wasn't worth knowing.

'There's all the difference between nipping and biting,'

he answered my eyes full of question marks. Not immediately appreciating this distinction, I mentioned I thought a hard dog could develop into a vicious dog, a hunter rather than a herder, and finish up being more a hindrance than a help.

He agreed, took a long hard look at Happy, and said: 'She's young enough yet awhile to be corrected. Let her know who's boss. She'll learn.' I confessed my dilemma about how to control her aggression without undermining it completely, turning her into a soft dog with no interest in the sheep generally, let alone the tough ones which required firm handling.

'Let her know who's boss,' he repeated. 'Next time she nips or holds on throw something at her.' He chuckled. 'She'll soon get the idea.' He stooped to pick up a handful of mud. 'This'll do, not too soft,' his eyes twinkled. 'Each time she deserves it let her have it. If there's no mud about,' he wiped his hand on the grass, 'try a bit of rubber tubing.'

During the next training session, perhaps because the sheep appeared so obliging, we had no trouble; but the one after Happy again forgot herself, helping an obstinate ewe on its way with more than a nip. My mud was ready. Shouting 'No' at the top of my voice I let fly. And missed by a mile. Nevertheless Happy let go, and looked bewildered in my direction.

'Here,' I screamed, almost as much out of control as the dog. Unhesitatingly she responded, and sat expectantly at my feet. The obstinate ewe re-joined the others and all six, given a five-minute respite, appeared far less agitated.

'Come bye,' I commanded. Happy raced away, made a perfect approach and gently brought the ewes on. 'Steady,' I shouted as she seemed to be getting too close to the one at the back. Happy responded, but not soon enough. At least the ewe panicked and shot off from the others. Alas, its backside proved irresistible to the dog, and she hung on tenaciously.

Fortunately from my standpoint the ewe swerved to offer me an easy target. Screaming 'No' my aim was reinforced by my exasperation. The mud hit Happy on the ear and cascaded round her face. She let go immediately, looked astonished, and didn't need telling twice to lie down.

It would be nice to report this was the termination of her uncontrolled aggression, but quite a few more excellent aims were required before she got the message completely. Not that she hasn't once or twice since had reason to assert her authority with a nip, but on those rare occasions she was, I think, largely justified.

Bill Wheel must have been giving a blow by blow account of Happy's training to old Fred, for the next time the cat lover saw me he asked about the biting, and mumbled something about not worrying too much about it. He seemed subdued, so unlike his normal jovial self.

I enquired about the missing tom. 'Yes, he came back after six weeks. No idea where he'd been or why he returned after such a time. Walked into my shed,' Fred laughed for the first time, 'as large as life demanding to be fed, as though he'd never been away.'

The old man seemed on edge, happy to talk but himself saying little. I chatted about the farm and how much we were looking forward to the start of tupping on bonfire night, mentioned how well Bill's Jersey calf was doing, and half turned to go. 'I suppose you've heard?' he said.

Fred then told me of the other tom, son of the wanderer, and main reason why the number of half-wild cats on the allotment were getting out of hand. The RSPCA were sympathetic to Fred's request, but explained that to find good homes for cats was difficult at the best of times, especially, they gently underlined, untamed cats. The best thing in all the circumstances was, they advised, to have all nine put to sleep.

The old cat lover resisted, argued with himself, but finally was compelled to admit there was no other way. Arrangements were made for the RSPCA inspector to do the necessary at Fred's house in the village.

On the appointed day he went to his allotment and placed the cats excluding only tom the elder into a box. His home, Fred emphasized, was half a mile or three fields away.

One by one he held his snarling, spitting felines while the injection was given, and carried them to his back garden.

Tom the younger was last. Fred stroked him as the inspector re-filled the syringe. As the needle approached, the cat leapt from the caress, bolted through the kitchen door, and was last seen heading for the canal.

About a week later he nonchalantly strolled into the allotment shed, lovingly welcomed. 'What puzzles me,' Fred perked up, 'how did he know his way back? Remember, I put him in a box with the others; he couldn't see the way we went from the allotment to my house in the village.'

Fred didn't wait for me to unravel the mystery, even supposing I could. Recalling the fateful day in such detail was too much. Tears rolled down his unshaven cheeks as he climbed on to his bike, muttering something about never forgiving himself. I walked home through the woods, wondering again at the tender heart of a tough old boot like Fred.

Hearing the story, my wife recalled how when she was

a girl her mother found it necessary to give away the family cat, city born and bred. It was taken to its new home nine miles away deep in the country. Within days it was back. And this called to mind an unlikely story told to us both by an impeccable source.

The vicarage cat, a beloved of some eighteen years, went missing and her mangled body was discovered by the side of the road. Last rites were tearfully said, and it was many months before another cat was invited to fill the unfillable.

Months later still, a mangy cat meowed on the vicarage doorstep. The vicar and his wife couldn't believe it, yet to doubt was impossible. The old lady, their first love, risen from the dead.

Remarkable animals, cats! I should know. Fred tells me so every time he sees me.

There was nothing remarkable about the way Happy floundered in learning to drive the sheep *away* from me, the next item on our training programme. To drive them toward me was for her natural or instinctive; I was the pack leader to whom she was pushing the quarry, and furthermore she could see me, an easy focal point. But immediately I reversed the operation she was flummoxed.

I realize now that my lack of experience added to her confusion, just a little! For a start I didn't appreciate enough how difficult this manoeuvre was going to be. We'd made excellent progress with the six sheep generally speaking; Happy's aggression was definitely under control, and her response to my commands prompt, no messing. Already she was proving her worth in the day to day running of the farm, saving a lot of time and even more aggro, encouraging me blithely to imagine her competence was comprehensive. Then I wanted her to drive the flock away from me, and quickly discovered we were, as they say, into another ball game altogether.

Eventually she managed it, due largely to Bill Wheel as usual coming to the rescue. He advised me to run *with* the dog, behind her but sufficiently close to give her assurance as she kept the ewes within her sights. No need, he said, to worry about the ewes, they'll keep moving because of the dog. My job was simply to steady her nicely behind them but ahead of me.

Now on paper this doubtless seems elementary, but the reality I – never mind Happy – found less than straightforward. Either the ewes tended to scatter, encouraging the dog to revert to her normal practice of cutting them off and pushing them toward me, or she looked back too often for reassurance to maintain real control. For ages I tried to keep her central behind the ewes, calling her to left or right, and commanding her to lie down at the first sign of disorder, but progress was at best spasmodic and at times disheartening. Watching her now you'd never guess the trouble and despair.

What finally convinced me she'd got it together was a visit to a farm in the next village, result of a tip-off inevitably from Bill Wheel. A farmer he knew was selling up, retiring, Bill said, and his tegs were special at the right price.

When Happy and I arrived the farmer was affable enough, but his asking price made me wonder how Bill could have been so misinformed. No doubt, though, about the quality of the tegs. Inexperienced as I was, I could see they were first-class.

As things turned out there was no haggling. It was either his price or nothing, take it or leave it, not a chance of a reduction. To be honest I preferred this type of sale, a reflection, I suppose, of my ineptitude or

47

embarrassment at trying to knock down prices or more likely myself being pushed higher.

The one thing that really surprised me was the absence of a working sheepdog on the farm. Happy was with me, of course, but it never crossed my mind I'd have to use her. Surely the farmer would pen the tegs and transfer them to the transporter, in this case our trailer adapted for the purpose. He explained he'd already sold his two young sheepdogs; the only one left was a pet, long past her working days. His assumption was I wouldn't mind using my dog!

My heart sank. Working Happy within the privacy of our own farm was one thing, suddenly putting on what seemed to me a public display was something else. Yet there was nothing else for it. The tegs needed rounding up. I had a sheepdog. What were we waiting for?

Happy looked at me expectantly, sensing something was on. In a nervous voice strangely unlike my own I whispered *Come bye*, and she shot off to my left, making a beautiful approach to get right behind the sheep without agitating them in the least. Not waiting for any further command she brought them on, toward the gate where the farmer and I were watching, he with a life-time of experience, I hiding my apprehension.

Through the gate they trotted, Happy steady, keeping her distance like a practised veteran, the farmer and I strolling behind chatting as though neither of us had a care in the world. If things had gone wrong it would have been entirely my fault, for Happy took the sheep to the far side of the field, exactly where we wanted them to go, and only hesitated when she didn't know what to do next. The sheep bunched in a corner getting restive, a few of them milling around obviously looking for a way of evading the dog. I shouted to Happy to lie down, the farmer casually lifted back a hurdle to open a pen, and soon we were able to pick off my twelve without too much trouble.

I slipped the catch of the trailer into position, and called Happy to take her usual place with me in the front. 'She's a fine dog for a young 'un,' the farmer remarked, little realizing he'd just witnessed her first really competent performance, a giant step forward in confidence for both of us.

Happy and I were now virtually inseparable. As soon as I appeared in the kitchen at first light, she bestirred herself from her snug box by the Rayburn stove, and stood, tail wagging, waiting for me to make my way to the cowshed. Once there, she settled down patiently while I did the milking and fed the pigs. The only morning I remember any deviation was when I heard such goings on in my workshop next door, and Happy eventually emerged with a huge rat in her mouth. Still alive! She dropped it at my feet, and it scarpered for the door. In a flash Happy sprang after it, and this time offered no reprieve.

My feelings were not unmixed. Naturally I was glad to be rid of the rat, and delighted at Happy's lightning reaction, but Bill Wheel had warned me not to encourage her to chase rabbits, arguing that the last thing I wanted was an excitable dog charging off out of control possibly when she was working the flock; and presumably the same applied to rats.

'Let her know who's boss,' he endlessly repeated, meaning she must never be allowed to be a law unto herself, follow her instinct or not. If you want a ratter, he'd gone on to say, get yourself a Jack Russell, one of his own, he'd offered, but a sheepdog's sole job on a sheep farm was with the sheep. Allow Happy to think

49

otherwise, and she'd cause as much trouble as she was worth!

Fortunately rats were few and far between, doubtless due to our two monster farm cats whose hunting skills were matched only by their capacity to keep fighting fit despite over eating. Theoretically they were fed each morning in the farmhouse, along with our two confirmed domestic felines. In fact most mornings they couldn't even be bothered to come, so satiated were they after another successful night's hunting.

Fred the old cat lover thought they were magnificent, much to be preferred to the other two, not least, I think, because he claimed they shared a common lineage with his recently departed. Tom the elder was their grandfather, if not their father, Fred insisted, though how precisely this came about he never elaborated. The known facts certainly didn't corroborate Fred's story.

We were given the cats shortly after we arrived on the farm by a neighbour who warned us we'd be overrun by rats and rabbits if we didn't take precautions. He led us to a barn where we were greeted by half a dozen cats I for one wouldn't have liked to meet in the dark, and also about the same number of kittens. As we talked the farmer threw a rabbit he'd shot that day to the cats which reacted like a pride of lions at feeding time.

'Take a couple of kittens,' he said, 'they'll make marvellous farm cats, earn their keep in no time. As a matter of fact,' he laughed, 'just throw them the occasional rabbit, and they'll look after themselves.' Talk about understatement! Our two farm cats, now both so big it's hard to believe they were ever so tiny as the kittens we saw in our neighbour's barn, prowl about our farmyard and surrounds understandably keeping rodents of all shapes and sizes firmly under control, and growing fat and sleek in the process. About the only time they condescend to patronize my generosity is when I offer them the first half pint or so at morning milking. Usually they await my arrival, and stay for as long as their thirst is quenched. Then off they disappear to sleep off another night of gluttony.

They tolerate Happy with unconcealed affection. Let any other dog appear, and they react the opposite of intimidated, hunching their backs, spitting like a cobra, ready to pitch in if the stranger ventures too near. But with Happy, when they're not wholly indifferent, they nestle with her and have been known to start to lick her, an indignity she spurns.

I'm told cats are basically incapable of affection for human or beast, apart from themselves. Judging by the fierce independence of our hunting pair this is indisputable, but my wife disagrees. In the first place she says the farm cats are not so much felines as ferals, not to be confused with our two domesticated moggies whose aptitude for gracious living at least gives the impression of returned affection; and secondly she points to the way the ferals allow themselves to be fussed by the children.

Strangely enough my attitude to prowling cats began to change shortly after we received two pairs of doves from well meaning friends in the city. We erected the dovecot in our front garden, plus a sizeable enclosure to restrict the birds for three weeks to focus their new home.

At the end of this period I removed the enclosure and watched the doves disappear, not to return. That, we thought, was that. But a good twenty-four hours later, they swooped in not directly on to the dovecot but the roof of the farmhouse, all four of them, bang on target, not a flicker of hesitation. We reacted like excited children not able to believe their good fortune.

The next three weeks were idyllic. Doves playing around the farmyard, roosting in or on the dovecot, engaging in rituals of mating, endlessly cooing notably, we soon discovered, in the early morning; only those who haven't kept doves can think of them as symbols of peace.

We counted the days to the emergence of the first pair of fledglings. Out they came, the first one to be dispatched by a feral, the other to be thrown by me on to the farmhouse roof as a safety precaution. Once propelled upwards it opened its wings, and completed the journey without mishap.

So now we had five doves. Two months later seven. Soon it was nine, eleven, thirteen . . .

The doves continue to breed all the year round, snow on the ground or not. But for the ferals' ability to match both the birds' fecundity and my safety precautions we'd be overwhelmed.

How do you teach doves family planning? A farmer's wife up the road suggested we boil the eggs. No use, she insisted, removing them; the birds simply produced more. Boil them and put them back!

It seemed such a dirty trick, a con to encourage perfect futility. Yet how else to control their numbers? Is there a pill we could mix with their daily feed? We've tried giving them away, but invariably the enthusiastic response of would-be receivers peters out in the cold light of practicalities.

Fred the odd-job man suggested we should eat them. Forget the twin barriers of our sentimentality and how precisely to carry out the kill, he couldn't understand, himself an old age pensioner, why we disregarded this self-evident way to cheaper living. Otherwise, he said, leave it to the cats; in fact, listening to Fred, anybody would think we were denying the ferals their rightful dues. And I begin to think he's right.

Funny thing. I hated the way cats prowled on birds. Until we had doves.

I suppose that's a negative reason for liking cats. Liking? To be honest I don't like them any more than I dislike them. But I'm much more than indifferent. I admire them, the ferals anyway, for their hunting skills no less than their fastidious cleanness, their ability to look after themselves. The fact remains, it's almost impossible to have a relationship with a cat. Even our domesticated couple appear concerned only about regular feeding without effort, and their comfort. These provided they keep themselves very much to themselves, bestirring themselves for little more than to use the catflap for obvious reasons.

Happy is the absolute contrast. As soon as I appear in the kitchen at first light, she leaps from her snug box by the Rayburn stove, and stands, tail wagging, waiting for me to make my way to milking. Wherever I go on or off the farm these days she is rarely far away. On the farm she either walks to heel or jumps on the trailer or takes her now accustomed place at my feet in the tractor cab. Even off the farm I feel incomplete without her.

One Saturday morning, unable to sleep, I crept out of the farmhouse long before first light to walk in the woods on the boundary of our farm, my favourite place when I want to be on my own to think. As I passed through the farmyard our magnificent cockerel, still self-acclaimed king of all he surveys, prematurely heralded the dawn, perhaps prompted by belligerence toward me or the dog whose presence I hadn't noticed until then. You've no idea – or have you? – what a comfort her company provided.

Long before we reached them rabbits scattered into the woods, and by the time we were walking through shafts of moonlight from the trees total silence enveloped us. It was almost eerie. Occasionally I heard animals scurrying but saw nothing, otherwise stillness was near absolute.

We made our way to the part of the woods I know best, hoping for another glimpse of a fox or even badgers reported to be in the vicinity, but doubtless our walking warned them off long before we arrived. I realized soon after coming to the farm that the only way to see wild animals is to be still, become a silent part of their habitat, with plenty of patience simply to wait and watch. On this occasion – walking helping to concentrate my mind – the peace and quiet of the woods were reward enough.

Dawn was beginning to break, changing the appearance of the familiar as in the half-light some of the trees assumed grotesque forms while parts of others looked uncannily human helping me to appreciate why trees were once revered as final resting places for the souls of the departed.

Happy was lively but made no attempt to investigate anything, not even an owl that began to hoot nearby. Paradoxically this hooting like the mooing of a distant cow underlined the silence all around us.

Then it started, at this unearthly hour! For a moment I couldn't believe my ears, but the persistence of the whining turned my feet toward a part of the woods I rarely visited. And there in the distance was a man presumably testing his chainsaw. Standing under a tarpaulin on four poles, a primitive workshop or shelter, he revved it repeatedly before switching it off and turning to his main work of the day.

He picked up a length of wood, stripped it of bark, split it, and very soon a bundle of pales or palings was near complete, my first experience of such a craftsman at work. His speed was truly remarkable. 'We're a dying breed,' he said, 'the youngsters won't have it. Prefer the factory.'

He told me he liked to arrive at first light; an early start meant he was free to finish in the middle of the afternoon, his twenty bundles of twenty-five pales each completed. 'Nothing like being your own boss,' he smiled. 'Start when you like, finish when you like. No one to bother you. I come out here,' he looked round the woods, 'and normally don't see a soul all day. You get used to it,' he summed up.

'Never lonely?' 'Too much to do,' he continued stripping the bark, obviously happy to talk so long as it didn't interfere with output. He learned the craft from his father, he and his elder brother. The brother, now officially retired, still did a couple of days a week, when he felt like it, if the weather was kind. 'Gets him from under his wife's feet,' he laughed.

I suddenly remembered it was past time to do the milking. 'You'll get there all the quicker if you don't hurry,' he swung his knife not wasting a moment. 'Come and see me again,' he shouted as we reached the turning.

After milking and then feeding the pigs, we checked the flock, and I noticed a couple of ewes limping, one rather badly. Despite the obvious discomfort the cripple still ran with the others as Happy calmly pushed them into a corner of the field where it wasn't difficult quickly to identify the limper again. I moved in gently, grabbed a hind hock, and sat the ewe on her backside. Firmly wedged between her hoofs was a sharp stone already cutting deeply into the flesh. To remove it was easy, thanks to a shepherding penknife I always carried for a multiplicity of jobs, but to prevent infection was more problematic. I decided to bring forward one of the regular antibiotic foot baths for the whole flock, and trim their hoofs into the bargain. Better safe than sorry; and with footrot always a potential threat my maybe overcaution needed little encouragement.

After breakfast Happy and I drove the flock to a penned area leading to the single-file entrance to the foot bath. But first came the hoof trimming, a back breaking exercise even when the sheep were co-operative! One by obstinate one I grabbed and upended them, rendering their struggles futile by holding them firmly between my legs and snipping away. Some of the hoofs required little attention while a few had grown so much they were curling under the foot trapping dirt and encouraging disease.

Eventually the job was done, and I left Happy behind the flock to keep them moving steadily through the foot bath as I worked the separating race at the other end to pick off the three or four needing further treatment for footrot.

With these safely penned, Happy and I went to collect our two rams for the same hoof trimming and foot bath. She made a perfect circular approach behind them, one little more than a year old, the other almost four times that age. They came toward me, not the least suggestion of trouble, passed through the gate leading to the field with the penned area, and trotted ahead as meek as lambs, Happy eyeing them with evident relish.

At the entrance to the penned area, the older ram

decided to be awkward, and found himself trapped between Happy and a closed farmyard gate. Unhesitatingly he turned to face the dog and charged. Correction. He started to charge, head down, resolute. Happy didn't budge, not by a whisker. The ram tried again, this time stopping barely short of the dog, staring in astonishment, and finally lunging forward.

Happy snapped at the ram's nose. Whether she let go or was shaken off I'm not sure, but either way the ram speedily accepted defeat, darting to join the other ram, with Happy in pursuit. Within half a minute both rams were inside the pen, no further nonsense, presumably grateful for protection from the dog. And we've had little trouble with them since, though what happened on one unforgettable morning with the younger ram and Happy I'll leave to the appropriate part of the story.

Inside the pen, however, with only me to contend with, both rams developed a new level of bloody-mindedness, as determined to frustrate me as I was to grab and upend them. I might still have been there if it hadn't occurred to me to call Happy inside the pen to keep the rams preoccupied as I used my hock crook to pick them off.

All the activity on the farm, Happy's no less than the family's and mine, was geared to bonfire night. And not only because of the fireworks! Bonfire night was to mark the start of tupping, that time of merry-making when the rams were free to roam the flock. The gestation period for a lamb is 147 days, meaning if tupping started on bonfire night the first lambs could be expected on April 1st. This simple calculation, one of the first things I learned about sheep farming without forgetting, became the foundation for our lambing programme.

As bonfire night approached, the BBC kept telling us

to lock up our animals, doubtless a wise precaution, but we had the very opposite plan in mind. Our pair of rams, segregated from the flock, were increasingly impatient to earn their keep. One of the ways they relieved their frustration was to do battle with each other, pawing the ground like angry bulls, putting their heads down and charging full tilt. The thud as their skulls collided left me in no doubt about either their durability or strength. Catching sight or whiff of the sheep they became frantic, further evidence of their prime condition for the hectic weeks ahead; and as the sap continued to rise, their frustration sometimes presented difficulties.

Time after time Happy proved her worth, not least in keeping the randy pair suitably subdued as I fitted their raddling harness, a simple device to colour the rumps of the sheep as they were served. By periodically changing the colour from red to yellow to blue I would be able not only to see which sheep had received the ram but also to work out the order in which their lambs were likely to be born.

Preparation for tupping includes a sort of confidence trick on the ewes and tegs, all fair and above board, but still crafty. When I first heard about it, that is, the theory behind it, I suspected somebody was pulling my leg.

In a nutshell, the flock are first grazed on sparse pasture which compels them to work hard for a change to appease their hunger. This also explains why each time they see us anywhere near they rush in our direction baaing and bleating in ear-splitting proportions to make the point it's past their customary weekly transfer to new pasture. Sheep might be stupid but never when it comes to their stomachs!

Then, with three weeks still to go before bonfire night,

we move them to the extreme contrast – lush pasture carefully prepared, as much as they want. You can imagine their delight, like children let out early from school, hardly able to contain themselves. And by bonfire night itself they've just about eaten themselves into perfect condition for the ram. In other words, their bodies are instinctively reacting – with all this food about, we're safe to have at least twins, even quads!

Smile if you like, I tell you it works.

Shortly before the fireworks were due to start in more ways than one, the older ram decided his necessity couldn't wait. My first indication was a phone call from a neighbour asking did I realize one of our rams was chasing the flock next door? Not to worry, the kindly voice laughed, we've rounded him up; collect him at your leisure.

So Happy and I walked a reluctant ram back to his strictly male enclosure. To relieve his now unbearable impatience he immediately engaged in renewed combat with the younger ram whose tender age made him no less determined. Rams are not the most conciliatory of creatures, and just before tupping their normal objection to being handled is reinforced tenfold. Not surprisingly, therefore, their desperation to get at the sheep can sometimes test the bravest of sheepdogs, never mind the shepherd!

Happy and I, for instance, were moving the rams to a pen where I wanted to check their feet, incidentally only days after the previous examination. That morning I'd noticed one of them with what looked like a slight limp, and foot trouble during tupping specially for the rams could well prove disastrous. In any case, my now firmly established policy was better safe than sorry.

We collected them from their meadow and through a field adjacent to where the flock were grazing. All went according to plan until the elder caught sight of his lovelies. He made a beeline for the fence, ran along presumably looking for an opening before charging it again and again with the frenzy of a sex pervert.

Happy barely waited for any command. In a flash she was after the ram which nevertheless was too single-minded about other things readily to fall into line. Actually it looked for a moment as though he was prepared to transfer his venom against the fence to the dog. But this was before Happy nipped his backside, just the once. Afterwards a very obedient ram, still spasmodically feinting bold defiance, continued on course, wiser if even more massively frustrated.

In the pen it was comparatively easy to grab a hock, but to hold on against his vicious kicking and finally manage to upend him was another matter. By the time he was firmly between my legs, and helpless, he'd drawn blood, mine of course, and made it perfectly clear he had no intention of co-operating in anything.

The younger ram wasn't much easier; and as the feet of both, as far as I could see, were in excellent condition I wondered whether my caution was, after all, worth the trouble.

The day after bonfire night I counted several coloured bottoms, and daily their number increased. Soon red rumps bobbed all over the place, followed by blue or yellow, evidence of the rams' alacrity, promise of spring, enough to gladden the heart of any shepherd.

Mind you, some of the ewes also had red faces, outcome of the younger ram's virginal ineptitude! For having sniffed in the right place to convince himself a ewe was in season, he persisted in trying to mount her at the wrong end. Time after time. She stood patiently waiting for consummation, while he, obviously desperate to oblige, nipped to the front and engaged in abortive gymnastics which grew in frenzy until, knackered to no purpose, he dismounted, took a necessary breather, and started the same futility all over again. I'd heard of sex education for the young, but this was ridiculous. For starters I'd never remotely suspected that rams were sometimes lacking in instinctive know-how.

Anyhow, what finally broke this circle of frustration was a four-lamb ewe. Now I'm not claiming that she from her vast experience put him wise, not at all; all I'm saying is that after nearly a day of getting nowhere he was observed engaged in vigorous burnishing at the right end; and from that moment he never looked back, if you see what I mean.

What also pleased me was Happy's attitude to the flock. Apparently sensing their need to be undisturbed, she kept unprompted well in the background, and always moved with caution as though anxious to be inconspicuous whenever necessity took us near them. In fact, as things turned out, all the farm animals – even the belligerent cockerel no less than the pigs, calves, housecows and sheep – proved the least of our troubles in this autumnal colour and excitement. A far greater headache centred upon the farmhouse chimney!

As much as we liked an open fire we didn't often have one. Our Rayburn, apart from being superb for cooking, provides constant hot water which also heats the bathroom through a towel rail. In the lounge we have a paraffin heater; might sound primitive but in our experience paraffin doesn't smell at all if the nozzle is kept clean and the wick trimmed. Into the bargain the heater, very effective even in the coldest weather, is much cheaper to run.

Nevertheless we use our spacious open fireplace on special occasions – Christmas, birthdays and the like. So when a relative paid us a rare and unavoidably brief visit from a considerable distance we naturally decided a blazing welcome was essential. An hour before he was due we applied the match!

He was greeted by billows of smoke, thickening the already murky atmosphere, causing him half-choking to grope for a chair, and also urgently to inform us how to clear the air; inform us, incidentally, with all the authority of a life-time townee. His advice sounded less than convincing, but with a meal waiting to be served our befogged situation hardly justified argument.

I screwed up yesterday's paper, lit it, and threw the inferno up the chimney. Almost immediately it fell back, followed by a trickle of soot, and another almighty billow of black smoke.

I tried again, and this time the flaming torch remained out of sight. From the breast of the chimney came a sustained roar, and moments later before our unbelieving eyes fell a bird's nest the size of a dinner plate, burning like crazy. After such a beginning the visit was bound to be a success, despite the fact that spasmodic billows, altogether more gentle, underlined that part of the blockage remained. Beyond question, the chimney required sweeping with more than townee solutions.

Yes, but where these days, particularly in our isolated neck of the woods, to find a chimney sweep? I hadn't seen one for years before coming here, and had no reason to believe they still functioned at all in our rural setting.

As usual I shared the problem with Bill Wheel, fund of

all local information. 'What do you want a sweep for?' he confounded me. 'Sweep it yourself. Only two requirements,' he laughed at my astonishment, 'a nice sprig of holly tied to a hazel branch.'

The hazel, he explained, was sufficiently flexible to bend to the shape of the chimney, whatever the twists and turns, while the holly made the finest sweeper imaginable. My wife further surprised me by agreeing that the idea sounded reasonable.

So at the first opportunity Happy and I went in search of the craftsman in the woods. The tarpaulin looked the worse for wear, evidence of the appalling weather over recent weeks, but bundles of neatly tied palings indicated that production continued apace.

'The weather!' the leather face creased into a smile, 'not too bad. I never bother about it, take it as it comes, can't afford to be a fair-weather worker.' His knife flashed, the wood split from top to bottom. 'Few things hard work can't put right,' he maintained production.

I gathered he always worked in the open air. If he wasn't making palings, his main job, he was picking fruit, an annual change to which he looked forward like a holiday. 'Balances things out nicely,' he stripped away more bark. 'Fruit picking and this job – suit me down to the ground.'

He eyed me quizzically. 'We're a dying breed,' he reminded me, 'the youngsters won't have it, not enough money, too much hard work. Beats me,' the knife again flashed.

'Hazel!' he answered my request, 'marvellous stuff for hurdles and fishing rods; bends back on itself, no trouble at all.' I followed him deeper into the woods. 'Like this,' he grabbed a branch on a tree, and started to twist it in the middle. Within seconds he bent it double, repeatedly swinging it back on itself. Yet once released it shot back to its former position undamaged.

'They use hazel,' his running commentary continued, 'for thatching pegs; not really suitable for my job. If there's nothing else I use it but it's harder to strip the bark.' His order of preference was chestnut, by a mile, then ash, sycamore, maple, red birch (not white), and alder. 'Hazel's perfect for what you have in mind,' he reassured me, adding that sweeping a chimney with hazel and holly sprig was the traditional countryman's way, none better.

Darting from tree to tree, explaining why the branches he examined weren't suitable, he eventually found the ideal, two branches in fact. 'If this one,' he pointed to a lengthy piece, 'isn't long enough, tie it to this one.' The second was more substantial but shorter. Triumphantly I marched home, Happy at heel doubtless wondering what in the world was going on.

We decided, my wife and I, to tackle the chimney the following morning, immediately after she'd returned from taking the children to school. First we emptied the lounge of pretty well everything, then covered the immovable bits and pieces with newspaper, and finally again with newspaper stuffed every nook and cranny. Next, my wife enveloped her hair in a scarf the size of a shroud, in the event too prophetic by half, while I stripped apart from a pair of shorts theoretically no use for anything but dusters.

Already I'd cut the holly from an abundance at the garden gate, and tied it to the hazel. 'Ready?' I called to the laughing shroud. She gripped the bottom of the branch as we advanced. Now what did Bill and the woodman say? Hazel was pliable enough to snake its way anywhere, corners notwithstanding!

We pushed, pulled, twisted, heaved, charged, ramrod-ded – the chimney seemed solid. Finally we bent the branch almost ninety degrees, and shoved for all we were worth. Partial success was intoxicating. In a frenzy we positively attacked the chimney, and suddenly, lurching forward as something seemed to give, we were really on our way.

'Nip outside,' I laughed, 'to see if the holly's showing.' 'Keep pushing,' my wife kept calling. I did, but by the time she returned disappointed we were, I had not the slightest doubt, in not a little trouble. Not only had the holly refused to emerge, but I couldn't get it any higher. Or lower. We were stuck with barely a thimbleful of soot to show for our endeavours.

'Why not,' my wife sounded matter of fact, 'sweep the chimney from the top?' I was too exasperated to appreci-ate her sense of humour, but eventually was compelled to realize she wasn't trying to be funny, not one little bit. So having established that the holly, come hell or high water, was less inclined to go up than to come down, and having also almost done ourselves a mischief in trying to retrieve it, I climbed on to the roof, precariously received the extended hazel branch with renewed holly from her outstretched hand, nervously completed my journey to the chimney, and waited for her signal to plunge.

She checked the dust sheets, resumed her place at the fireplace, and shouted the all clear. In retrospect I realize I should have been less enthusiastic. Down came the holly at speed, accompanied by tons and tons, or so it seemed, of soot, overflowing the grate, defeating the dust sheet, settling on the newspaper and everything else within the farmhouse, a black cloud to harmonize with the face under the shroud. All that remained, apart from my hazardous return, was for the pair of us to clear up the mess.

Three begrimed hours later we revived ourselves with cups of coffee, and fond thoughts of our new sootlessness. Indeed, the chimney now sings like a love song. Only one thing continues to puzzle me. When, with the magnanimity of total success, we offered Bill the same impeccable service he mumbled something about the virtues of a suction pump.

In the country, I've noticed, there is an altogether more leisurely approach to life. It isn't that people don't work so hard, some would say the very opposite, but unhurried haste is as near panic as anyone gets. Life is meant to be lived, meaning enjoyed. Frantic activity of any sort is out of the question.

So when I saw a man digging a trench as though his life depended on finishing yesterday the sight was sufficiently unusual to warrant investigation. I should have known. He was a city dweller. The trouble was, he said, there were too many chiefs and not enough indians working for the council. Yes, but what was this to do with his frenzied digging? Other considerations apart, I didn't realize council workers were so conscientious.

He led me to his van, and pulled out an elaborate drawing specially prepared for this single job – a new ditch running the entire length of the road by the woods. 'Think of all the time they spent on this,' he pointed to the detailed drawing of the whole area, 'never mind a couple of them coming here to examine the job in the first place. And how long do you think they've given me to dig this trench, from there to here,' his hand spanned a hundred yards, 'twelve inches deep and twenty wide? Go on,' he repeated, 'how long?'

I began to calculate. 'Sixteen hours!' His exasperation couldn't wait for an answer. 'Imagine, sixteen!'

Looking at the distance and the mud and the two tree stumps directly in the way, I couldn't believe – despite the old country maxim: 'Set yourself more than you can do and you'll do it' – that any human with nothing but a spade was capable of digging such a trench in the time.

'Could you,' he played his trump card, 'do it in sixteen hours?'

As he folded the drawing every minute of his fifty-eight years protested that he couldn't wait for retirement. 'Think of the cost of all those chiefs planning this job, and then deciding,' his venom renewed itself, 'deciding I can do this lot on my own in sixteen hours! In this day and age! We put men on the moon, and I'm given a spade to dig a trench this long. How can you take pride in your work when you're beaten before you start? A mechanical digger could do the job in five minutes.'

His wellington boots sucked into the mud as he heaped out another spadeful, some of it splashing on his face and pullover. I genuinely felt sympathetic. After two full and weary days, working alone, thoroughly demoralized, the poor chap was barely half way.

Happy and I walked on intending to make our way through the wood back to the farm, a favourite short cut, but a familiar van horn heralded the arrival alongside of Bill Wheel. He wound down the window, characteristically taking his time and saying nothing, simply staring at the dog in his knowledgeable not to say critical way. Ignoring my greeting he kept looking, as though puzzled or unsure about something.

'She's doing well,' my embarrassment and growing concern broke the long silence. Bill continued to stare at Happy, his eyes penetrating. 'Are you free tomorrow morning?' he sounded casual. I hesitated, on my guard, inexplicably alarmed. 'There's an old shepherd friend of mine I'd like you to meet,' Bill drawled on, 'knows everything about sheepdogs. He'd be interested in your bitch.' Eventually it also emerged that Bill was going primarily to lend a hand repairing a sagging cowshed roof – and could do with an extra pair of hands!

We went in Bill's van, driving the ten miles or so through glorious scenery and finally along narrow lanes really deep into the country; the farm was tucked away paradoxically on the brow of a hill. Within minutes of arriving we were sipping coffee with the shepherd and his wife, both nearer eighty than seventy, either side of their kitchen table, a picture of contentment.

Making conversation I mentioned the disgruntled council worker and his impossible target. 'It's all those bureaucrats with their regulations and bits of paper,' the old man's eyes flashed. 'Hear that chainsaw! That's my neighbour, a woodcutter all his life. The other day a man with a form pitched up and told him he'd have to wear a tin hat at work. "A tin hat?" said my neighbour. "What do I want to wear a tin hat for?" "It's in the regulations,' threatened the official.'

'Not like the old days,' the shepherd's wife chipped in, 'we were left to get on with it then. But now,' she looked heavenwards, 'you need to fill in a form to say your prayers.'

Mention of the old days led them merrily to reminisce about their early married life, the time they didn't have a couple of coppers to rub together. His father, a nurseryman noted for his roses, suggested the newly-weds should take on the almost bankrupt other side of his business – a small dairy herd with a milk round three times a day.

At four o'clock each morning they climbed out of their

marital bed, he to do the milking by hand, she the bottling, for the first delivery to be on the doorstep by six. To be only minutes late was to risk losing customers to fierce competitors.

'We were never late,' the old shepherd bubbled, 'the pair of us worked all hours of the day and half the night – for years.'

'We were happy,' she said, not, I thought, without nostalgia.

'Hard work,' he spoke with the authority of someone who rises every morning at six, does a full day on the farm, and plans for the future with the enthusiasm of a youngster, 'hard work never did anybody any harm. That's the difference,' he sucked on the words, 'between working for yourself and digging a trench to somebody else's tune.'

'Do you know,' his wife suddenly changed the subject, her eyes full of mischief, 'what he gave me for my birthday?' His head dropped as he tried to hide behind his mug of coffee. 'Half a ton of coal,' her tone accused. 'That's right, half a ton of coal – for my birthday. And one year,' she was now in full flight, 'he bought me, would you believe, a new kitchen sink. For my birthday!'

'I couldn't think of anything else,' he laughed at himself, 'you've got everything you want.'

'Yes, but half a ton of coal!' she affectionately mocked.

The old sheep farmer, incidentally now the owner of his farm plus two others in the area, decided the time was long overdue to repair the cowshed roof. Happy followed as we picked our way through the mud to a byre not far from the farmyard where my main contribution to the job in hand was to pass tools and the occasional piece of wood as Bill and the old man jacked up the roof, a delicate operation requiring more brains than brawn, though still plenty of the latter.

Meanwhile the worker in the farmhouse kitchen was baking a steak and kidney pie, to have dinner on the table at twelve o'clock sharp, daily habit of their fifty odd years of married life.

Happy, not stirring or making a sound, sat under the table at my feet, totally ignored by the old shepherd who talked mainly about Spot his sheepdog which in fact, he explained, stopped working sheep a couple of years ago. With the entire flock now shepherded by a married daughter at one of the other farms, Spot's job was to herd cattle – bullocks up to the age of two years plus milkers each suckling three calves, their own and others purchased at market. I wondered whether the market calves were always readily accepted at the teat?

'Sometimes the milkers have to be educated,' the old man replied, poker faced.

'He means,' his wife piped up, 'they have to be shown the stick.'

Chuckling, making no concession to his indigestion, he pushed his chair from the table, and led the way to what he called the farm workshop. Spot was on her feet in a moment, plainly delighted with so much company, expecting to work and impatient to start. Ears pricked, eyes riveted, she followed the old man at heel, picture of a dog under perfect control.

If he gave a command I didn't hear it, but she was off like a rocket to herd her charges to pasture three fields away. No panic, no hassle; the cattle appeared to know precisely what was required of them as the dog, not too close, kept them moving through the farmyard and the first gate, never for a moment taking her eyes off them, working, as far as I could see, entirely on her own.

The bull, magnificent looking, needed no more persuading than the others. Meekly he fell into line, the dog in total command. As I watched this unhurried competence I had to admit to myself that Happy wasn't in the same class. Spot did nothing that Happy couldn't have done, or so I believed, but there was a polish about this performance I'd seen before only on TV. The difference was between a first and second class athlete, underlined perhaps most of all as Spot compensated for her master's oversight. Told to drive on, she promptly went back to collect a bullock he'd overlooked on the blind side of the byre. I was, as you can imagine, very impressed, and compelled to see Happy's undoubted progress in rather a new light. Maybe, after all, I didn't have the finest sheepdog in the world!

The old shepherd wasn't done yet. Unashamedly proud of his dog, and deciding the occasion called for a comprehensive demonstration of her or their skills, he sent Spot to separate the bull from the herd and return him to the farmyard. The burly creature wasn't impressed. This time he turned to face the dog, and threateningly lowered his massive head.

Spot held her ground, no suggestion of backing off, silently asserting her authority to such an extent that the bull clearly reluctantly fell into line. 'She wouldn't have found one of my earlier bulls that easy,' the old man laughed, and went on to explain how it had once cornered a herdsman, causing him to run for his life. After that, the man refusing to go anywhere near it, the beast had to be sold. Getting it to market had been straightforward enough, but persuading it to leave the transporter for display at the sale had finally defeated everybody. Bill found this unbelievable, and made no attempt to hide his contempt. 'He could be a wicked brute,' the old man emphasized; 'in the end it had to be sold in the waggon.'

All this time Happy watched, apparently taking everything in, careful to keep not more than a stride away from me. She seemed nervous, subdued, as though intimidated by the excellence of Spot's performance. Actually I was feeling rather subdued myself. Until now my impression was that Happy's training and response were satisfactory, even encouraging, but seemingly I'd overrated both. I still believed she was an above average dog, but Spot's capability confronted me with the near impossible standard of TV's One Man and His Dog, a standard I thought miles removed from ordinary farming. Yet here was an unsung dog in an excessively muddy farmyard operating with enough style to cut both Happy and me down to size.

'Well, come on,' the old shepherd addressed me, 'let's see what your dog can do.' I wanted the ground to open up, and looked appealingly to Bill. Highly amused, he put his arm round my shoulder, and admitted this was why he'd brought me in the first place – he wanted to know what his old friend thought of Happy.

To say I hesitated is a blatant understatement. I panicked. My legs trembled. My heart thumped. Reflecting my feelings, Happy herself slunk to the ground at my feet, no more keen to work than I to work her.

The old shepherd briefly looked at me, then hard and long at the dog. 'Do you think,' he challenged, 'she could return the bull to the herd?'

Instantaneously there flashed to my mind Happy's early encounter with the hoof. Since then I'd seen to it that she kept a respectful distance from the housecows, not that she'd needed any prompting from me. As far as I could judge, Happy's herding instinct was focused exclusively on sheep. In any case, on a farm like ours using her with cattle hardly applied.

I mumbled something to this effect, but the old man's only response was once more to stare at the dog, and casually insist it was about time she was showing what she was made of. 'She'll be all right,' Bill assured me, adding belatedly, 'if she's any good.'

I glanced at the bull. It was huge, a veritable colossus, meek or not. Encouragingly Happy was by now lively on her feet, eyes bright, looking at me expectantly, obviously aware something was doing. The old shepherd, Spot behind him, and Bill waited, not impatiently but offering me no means of escape.

I chickened out. Another look at the bull convinced me. I was asking too much of such a young and relatively inexperienced dog. It was plain commonsense not to expose her in this way. Yet in a voice strangely unlike my own I heard myself whispering *Come bye* – and she was away.

Her approach was fine, perhaps not wide enough given the circumstances, but totally effective. The bull began to move toward the farmyard gate. Happy pushed him on, firm, steady, creating the impression she was accustomed to working cattle. I called her to the right, and, never taking her eyes off the bull, she responded immediately. No trouble, through the gate they went and into the adjacent field, still two removed from the herd.

The three of us followed, Spot walking to heel without command, I with my heart in my mouth, the other two chatting unconcernedly to each other. Happy and the bull approached the final gate. By now, despite an autumnal nip in the air, I was perspiring, and longing for the gate to be closed behind the bull. He sauntered forward, apparently ignoring the dog, concerned only to re-join his lovelies. Why he suddenly took it into his head to stop, peer over his shoulder, and turn to face Happy I shall never know. The whole operation took place in gentle slow motion, suggesting the bull wasn't so much obstreperous or angry as determined to make a point.

The dog momentarily stopped before creeping forward, her eyes boring into the bull. Likewise the bull glared at the dog, lowered its head and feigned a charge. Happy crouched low, not backing off even slightly. Again the bull feigned a charge. The two animals, a picture of transfixed belligerence, were not more than three strides apart. Then the bull swung round and trotted through the gate, as submissive as a pet poodle.

The old shepherd was like a man who'd won the pools, while Bill murmured something about he'd always believed Happy was a good 'un. I started to breathe again, and called the dog for the fussing she richly deserved. At the same time, though, let me be honest and admit I also felt guilty. As much as I was delighted with my dog, I believed I shouldn't have subjected her to such a test. I was a coward not to have refused.

For all that, there was no holding the old man's delight, and this, of course, quickly eliminated my secret reservations. 'I knew she could do it,' he enthused, 'she's got guts, character. Without *that*,' he almost shouted, 'you'd make nothing of her.'

We walked back to the farmhouse, the two dogs at heel, neither of them, I noticed, altogether easy with the other. Spot, big by comparison with Happy, was too disciplined to give vent to aggression, but otherwise her self-evident resentment at another dog receiving so much of the old man's attention could, I think, have turned nasty. As for Happy she kept closer to me than usual, making no attempt to hide her nervousness which in the

74

light of her recent display of courage surprised me. And it didn't help Spot's feelings, I'm sure, when she was dismissed to her kennel in the farm workshop, while Happy was allowed to accompany me indoors.

Waiting for us were scones hot from the oven, with strawberry jam and home-made cream. After the steak and kidney pie, never mind the trauma of the previous thirty minutes or so, I wasn't remotely hungry, but the old shepherd and Bill were no less enthusiastic about eating than singing Happy's praises. Bill in fact behaved out of character, heaping approval on the dog without caution or reservation.

Naturally I wallowed in the occasion. Yet something nagged at the back of my mind, refusing to go away. If the old shepherd was such an expert sheepdog handler, and I myself had seen enough evidence to eliminate doubt, what in the world was he doing exposing Happy to the possible aggression of the bull? I waited for what I hoped was the right moment before asking him.

He looked at me quizzically, his eyes a mixture of merriment and rebuke. 'You,' he wagged his finger, 'knew the dog. I knew the bull.' He laughed. 'For all his appearance he couldn't knock a fly off a rice pudding. I wanted to see your dog working; the bull needed returning to the herd. Seemed reasonable enough to me.' He winked at Bill, and helped himself to another scone. I wasn't entirely persuaded, and this must silently have communicated itself.

'Never, never, never,' he was suddenly solemn, almost aggressive, 'ask the dog to do too much.' He paused. 'At the same time,' his eyes were fierce, 'never, never, never, ask the dog to do too little.'

The old man looked at Happy, and smiled approval. 'Have you thought of entering her for novice sheepdog trials?' he asked. My reaction assumed he was pulling my leg, whereupon his wife tenderly rounded on me for having such a poor opinion of my own dog. I protested the opposite was the case, but this didn't blind me to Happy's limitations particularly after watching Spot at work. All the more reason, the old shepherd surprised me, to enter for the trials.

In the lively discussion that followed both he and his wife argued that this was the best way to guarantee the dog's development. For with such a goal I'd work harder at fundamental skills, and as the day of the competition approached my rising excitement, make no mistake, he insisted, would communicate itself to the dog and incidentally lift the tone of our routine chores together on the farm.

By the time we said our farewells I was almost persuaded to have a go. The one thing, let me be honest, that made me hesitate was my fear of making a fool of myself. Even so, I couldn't get away from the old man's insistence that sheepdog trials were themselves a useful part of a young dog's *training*. I'd always thought of them as part of a dog's testing, culmination of training, but the old couple were equally adamant that sheepdog trials trained as well as tested, especially novice sheepdog trials.

And, they chorused, they should know! Until his sixties the old shepherd had run his dogs at trials, and had never doubted the benefits whether they were placed or not. His wife, as open as a book, said they'd never won anything – a couple of seconds, but never a first. Nevertheless, they remained convinced that a young sheepdog with the promise of Happy had everything to gain, placed or not, and nothing to lose. I wanted to believe them.

The idea appealed so much, but I couldn't easily forget the occasions when Happy had scattered the sheep, bitten a few backsides, and in the general mêlée been indifferent to my commands. She was still young, little more than a year, and by comparison with Spot undeniably mediocre. At the same time I was not unimpressed by the old shepherd's bold assertion that she was not only worth running in trials but stood a fair chance of being placed. My inclination was, understandably enough, to take this with a big pinch of salt; but supposing, I kept asking myself, the old man was right!

What added paradoxically to my uncertainty was the reaction of the family. One mention of the idea, and they were already wondering where to display first prize in the farmhouse. Nothing more guaranteed. Happy was at least as good as the competitors in One Man and His Dog. Indeed, why not, they asked, enter for *that* competition? 'You'll be on the telly,' the children were irrepressible.

I still wasn't sure. True, I sent for details of novice trials within twenty miles, and eventually filled in an application form for the second one of the coming season, but even when I posted it the thought uppermost was that I could always withdraw even at the last moment. No need to make up my mind yet, merely get the application in by the deadline. But having got this far, I knew in my bones there was no going back. And as additional fuel to the blazing bridge behind me Happy began to perform with consistent efficiency.

Bill Wheel was hardly encouraging. He had nothing against sheepdog trials, you understand, but unlike his brother, something I was to appreciate increasingly, thought them 'a bloody waste of time'. As for Fred the cat man he was too busy trying to sort out the sudden increase in his ferals to show more than passing interest. What baffled him was the tom responsible, for his younger tom was again missing, not seen for ages, and the elder, he reluctantly conceded, was well past it. 'I know every cat in this area,' he said, 'and there isn't a tom that hasn't been cut.'

On the farm itself it was gladdening to see all the red, yellow or blue bottoms rubbed on the ewes by the rams as we continued to supplement winter grazing. I've mentioned before that sheep are controlled by nothing more than their stomachs. It's possible to pull the wool over their eyes in most things, but never when their feeding is involved.

Each morning I loaded the trailer with hay, and with Happy in her usual position in the tractor cab drove to renew supplies. Long before we arrived the sheep were responding to the time switch in their bellies, baaing and bleating with enough impatience to wake the dead; and as we passed through the gate the entire flock, jockeying for position at the head of the queue, followed after the fashion of the Pied Piper of Hamelin.

This daily exercise represented a conflict between the sheep's greed and their instinct to keep clear of the dog. The result was a sort of compromise – they neither ate nor ran, just milled around in a frenzy until one end of the feeder was packed, and Happy and I moved along to pack the remainder with the still sweet smelling reminder of hay making. As I stuffed in the nourishment, coloured rumps dashed this way and that, the whole flock seeking to pour, as it were, a pint of hunger into a half pint of space. Not until Happy and I were well out of the way did they settle with any degree of belligerent co-operation.

One morning, the hay renewed, I climbed back into the tractor, and only noticed as I slipped into gear that Happy wasn't in her usual place. Mystified or rather annoyed, I called her name repeatedly. Not a sign of her anywhere! She appeared to have disappeared into thin air.

It crossed my mind she might have run off, for only the week before the farmer from whom I'd bought her was telling me that her mother had recently taken to disappearing for a day or two, but I knew in any case that this was out of the question while the dog was working. There had to be another explanation.

As I continued to repeat her name she appeared over a slight incline at the far end of the field, came on a few spaces, started to bark, and turned back. In retrospect I realize how slow I was on the uptake, but it never immediately occurred to me she was trying to attract my attention to something. Even with the remembrance of Spot's initiative in working independently of the old shepherd to retrieve a bullock on his blind side of the byre, working in open defiance of her master's command, I still didn't cotton on to what Happy was about. On the contrary I walked towards her fuming at this new degree of disobedience.

For her part, she continued to appear and disappear over the incline, spasmodically barking, totally indifferent to my heated commands. I started to run, and with the dog now in view on both sides of the incline noticed what was clearly a sheep lying on the ground. It looked lifeless, but as I drew nearer its feet began frantically to beat the air like distress signals, reminding me of my first sight of a sheep similarly unable to help itself. It was, in fact, one of my neighbour's, and barely alive when I came across it. I heaved it to its feet, but the wretched creature, already one eye pecked out doubtless by crows, couldn't stand and died within minutes. Its other eye or rather

79

complete side of its head, rubbed raw by its prolonged struggles, was a dreadful mess.

'They get down,' my neighbour dismissed my concern, 'and can't get up; no foothold, you see.' Obviously my face expressed my bewilderment. 'Uneven ground,' he went on, 'feet going with the incline, leaves 'em stranded. They haven't the sense to move their arses a bit; just keep kicking the air searching for leverage.'

At the time, still quite new to farming ways, I found this a bit hard to take. I mean, sheep lie down all the time. What guarantee was there that any of them wouldn't find it impossible to get up?

The patient farmer smiled at my inexperience. 'It doesn't happen all that often,' he assured me, 'and when it does we usually spot 'em in time.'

Well, all I can say is that without Happy I wouldn't have spotted this one! Fortunately it hadn't been stranded too long. Immediately I grabbed it to its feet it shot off apparently none the worse for the experience, and joined the rugby scrum at the feeder.

When I told Bill his face reflected pity bordering on patronage. The sheep are silly buggers, he said, but surely you know the difference between a sheepdog's instinct and intelligence! The instinct works in harmony with the shepherd, the dog's pack leader; the intelligence occasionally prompts disobedience of the shepherd for *his* benefit. If you tell the dog to do one thing, and she does another, before you lose your temper, he laughed, find out why. I've had ample cause since to recall Bill's words.

Looking back I have no doubt that Happy's discovery of the prostrate sheep strengthened my resolve about the novice trial. Since posting my letter of enquiry the event had hung over me like the sword of Damocles. One moment I was wildly optimistic, the next certain I was inviting disaster of my own stupid making.

What really clinched the matter was a hand-written note from the secretary of our area sheepdog society. Don't be put off, he wrote, by understandable nervousness. We all have to start before we feel ready! In any case, you have the rest of the winter and early spring to prepare your dog.

My aim was to use these intervening months to work a replica course in our small meadow. But first I had to build it! Bill had a word with his brother, and the next thing I knew this total stranger arrived at the farm to lend a practical hand.

Country people have a reputation for excluding newcomers for years, outcome of inbred horse sense, but this wasn't our experience. From virtually the moment we arrived they rallied round not only in speaking a welcome but constantly turning their words into deeds. Nothing seemed too much – or too little – trouble.

Bill's brother arrived with his dog, or one of them, explained precisely what was required, helped to get up the gates, and emphasized the points for which the judges would be watching by running the course with his own dog, a vastly experienced bitch which made it all seem so easy.

What impressed me most, though, was the attitude of the handler. It's hard to put into words, but what I can only call his strong gentleness toward the dog somehow asserted his authority without stifling her initiative. Would Happy and I, I wondered, ever be capable of such a performance? And my forebodings weren't lifted as we attempted our first run. It's better I draw a veil over the whole episode.

As much as work on a one-man farm allowed, Happy and I returned to the makeshift course, seeking to develop the skills underlined by Bill's brother as being crucial for point scoring, but most of her training was centred upon routine activity on the farm. And this sometimes brought into sharper focus my inability consistently to control Happy's enthusiasm.

Now I've mentioned before that enthusiasm in a sheep-dog is essential; without it you're beaten before you start, if you ever get that far. But too much of this desirable quality creates disorder out of order. Shortly after the visit of Bill's brother, for instance, we were penning the sheep for a routine foot inspection. The morning was crisp and peaceful, the kind that sets the blood tingling and illustrates the privilege of country living.

I strolled along, not a care, responding to the loveliness all around, confident I could leave what was required to the dog. It must be difficult, I thought, to wash without hands! A blackbird was douching itself at a puddle – raising its soft feathers, spreading its wings, wringing itself with shakes and shimmies before plunging again.

The washing was terminated rather than concluded by the approach of a car driven by my wife. Either too preoccupied or prepared to dice with death, the bird continued splashing around. The driver, obviously expecting the bird to leave the puddle on the heavily pitted farm track, kept slowly coming. Only at the last possible moment did it get out of the way, twittering a massive protest.

The sheep and Happy long forgotten, I couldn't help but reflect on how animals generally keep themselves clean, most of them without the aid of water. It brought to mind my overhearing a neighbour asked by a group of children visiting his farm on a school project how often he washed his two sheepdogs. The farmer was in something of a quandary, having just looked suitably impressed when the questioner, clearly dotty about his dog, mentioned he bathed it fortnightly.

The children waited. The farmer looked at his sheepdogs, both beautifully clean, relief only slowly spreading over his face. 'I wash my dogs,' he announced, 'as often as some of you wash your cats.'

'But I never wash my cat,' piped up a little girl.

'Cats keep themselves clean,' the children shouted in chorus.

'Just like my dogs,' the farmer hurried to his cowshed, the children still looking not entirely convinced. His two dogs, by the way, are never allowed indoors. Never. Yet I've never seen them looking other than a picture of health. And their smell, whatever the weather and other contingencies on the farm, is never less than, well, reasonable.

Like most pigs I know! Before moving here I thought pigs were the dirtiest of animals, skunks included. As a lad my mother often told me I made my bedroom look like a pigsty. A problem family in our street were castigated for living like pigs; in fact, as not fit to live with pigs.

Yet when I saw how pigs really live, their sleeping space notably kept unfouled, I realized that my mother's intended insult was both a compliment to me, and an unjustified slur on the pigs. Their eating habits are another matter, but let no one tell me they're not clean. I speak what I know. As sweet as new mown hay!

Suddenly my reverie like the peace of the morning was shattered by three or four sheep darting past. The others quickly followed, and soon the whole bunch were going hell for leather in the direction from which we'd come.

Happy didn't hang about. She hurled herself at the trailing sheep, nipped quite a number of bottoms, hung on a couple of times, and succeeded only in scattering the flock. My frenzied commands were a waste of time.

Eventually, order restored, we completed the penning as though the interlude had never happened; and, telling myself it wasn't the dog's fault but mine for taking too much for granted, I resolved to keep my mind on the job. But Happy's regression to tendencies and behaviour long imagined remedied caused me again seriously to question the reasonableness of preparing her for novice trials. The whole idea seemed a sick joke.

Perhaps this was why initially I responded so unenthusiastically to an idea from Fred the cat man, that we should have another puppy. But first I had to hear his own important news. Tom the elder was dead, doubtless from old age, but tom the younger, having yet again returned after another mysterious disappearance, had immediately made his presence felt.

The rat was this size, Fred measured out the length on his arm, the biggest he'd ever seen. Young tom had already dealt with the mother rat and her brood, but her mate had proved too crafty. And even when eventually cornered near the allotment shed the giant rat had fought like a tiger.

Fred said he'd watched with his heart in his mouth, not sure at times his beloved tom would triumph. The rat had snapped its jaws on the cat's nose, and wouldn't let go. The old man had tried 'to hit the bloody thing with a stick', but the tom, apparently incensed at such humiliating intervention, had shaken himself free, and after much more spitting and fur flying killed the monster.

'What a cat!' Fred oozed with pride; 'and to think I

nearly had him put down.' The remembrance was clearly too unbearable to contemplate for more than a moment. Quickly he went on to itemize tom's injuries, a list as long as your arm including one ear almost severed, and a swelling on the nose as big as an egg. Innocently I inquired what the vet thought?

Fred's eyes filled with disbelief. The vet! whoever heard of a feral tom needing a vet? The deep cuts had healed almost as soon as the swelling had disappeared. Still chuckling the cat lover turned his bike and prepared to mount. By the way, he glanced over his shoulder, do you want another puppy?

My surprise must have registered with Fred as interest, for once more he turned his bike and stood staring at me, his eyes full of good news. A friend of his knew a farmer two villages away whose prize dog had just whelped. If I had any sense, Fred sounded solemnly light-hearted, I'd get another sheepdog in case anything happened to Happy. You never know! he gave the impression of certain disaster. And off he went, not trying to hide his despair at my indecision.

It must have been almost a week later that a blue van splashed its way along our deeply pitted farm track, and at the farmyard out stepped Bill Wheel, a dewdrop hanging precariously from his nose, while one of his Jack Russells yapped with enough venom to send the hens running; even the cockerel looked uncertain of himself.

As usual Bill unhurriedly rolled himself a cigarette casually looking around, showing not the slightest interest in me or any purpose of his unexpected visit. I watched him light his fag, re-light it, and typically spit out a strand of tobacco. The silence was deafening.

One of his cows, he eventually muttered, was again in calf. Was I interested? I was. The price? Bill asked how Happy was coping on the trial course, and as an afterthought mentioned how impressed his brother had been with her promise. 'He knows what he's talking about,' I was unnecessarily reminded, 'at least,' Bill laughed, 'about sheepdogs.'

As he prepared to wind himself back into the van, I told him, making conversation more than anything else, about Fred's idea of another puppy. His reaction amazed me. This normally placid man whose whole approach to life was the opposite of overt enthusiasm, suddenly became animated as I named the farmer whose dog had whelped. Making it clear I was a 'bloody fool' to have missed such an opportunity, he became literally hopping mad, transferring his weight from one leg to the other, apparently incapable of standing still in agitation. 'They will have all gone by now, whelps of that quality,' he revealed a side of his nature I'd never met before. By the time he left ten or so disgruntled minutes later I really believed I'd missed the chance of a lifetime.

But on reflection during another afternoon of ditching, and having again talked the matter over in the farmhouse, I confirmed to myself we didn't want a second dog, not yet. Happy was more than adequate for work on a farm like ours, and her training was taking all the time I could justify. A second sheepdog was a luxury we could well do without.

That firmly decided I was checking the calves when a revving engine indicated the arrival of Bill's van for an unprecedented second time in a day. Furthermore he actually hurried toward me in the barn, remarkable in itself, without for the first time in my experience either a cigarette in his mouth or a cigarette tin in his hand.

'There's one left,' he shouted, 'just the one. I've told the farmer to keep it for you.'

Now I'd heard of take-over bids, but this was ridiculous, not least because of Bill's expectation I would immediately drop everything to clinch the deal. My insistence that I do the milking first was as near as we'd come to an argument, and looked at one point like straining our relationship permanently. What baffled me was the extent of Bill's concern, not to say interference. True enough, often since I'd bought that first Jersey calf from him he'd placed his vast farming and country knowledge at our disposal, but never on a more than please yourself basis. On this occasion he was like a crusader, demanding action before it was too late, as though somehow *his* well being as well as mine depended upon the outcome. Irritation began, I fear, to settle on us both. Bill finally left with my assurance I'd at least go to look at the dog.

My wife and children accompanied me on the ten miles or so drive. Happy was with us, but we left her in the car as we made our way to the farmhouse. A knock was unnecessary. Waiting at the door to greet us was a middle-aged woman typifying the traditional farmer's wife. Exactly what I mean by this I find it hard to say, but one look at the woman in the doorway, and she had to be a farmer's wife. She invited us in, giving every indication she was expecting us to collect the puppy! There was no sign of her husband.

The kettle was singing on the hob. She made a pot of tea, cut slices of home-made fruit cake, and suggested to her teenage son he might like to show the children his angora rabbits. 'My husband won't be long,' she said, 'he's checking a cow in calf; she should drop it today.'

The waiting, longer than expected, didn't notice because an aspect of farming we'd never really thought about before cropped up. Holidays! Making it sound the most natural thing in the world she said that she and her husband hadn't been on holiday since their honeymoon twenty-three years ago. And even then they'd returned early after five days, he impatient to get back to the farm, she to take up her role as farmer's wife from her background of city life and nursing in a general hospital. She admitted they took single days at the seaside, after morning milking, of course, and back in time for afternoon milking at three thirty, otherwise even public holidays were ignored. 'When God commanded one day's rest in seven,' she laughed, 'he was obviously short on farming experience. In any case,' she couldn't have sounded more unanswerable, 'where could we go to anywhere nicer than here?'

Her husband left most of the talking to his wife as we drank tea, and the children finished off the cake. They'd returned excited saying the angoras were soon to have babies, and could they buy a couple? The farmer's wife's jocular warning that angora rabbits needed combing every day, and weren't worth the trouble, was hotly denied by her son, both the combing and the trouble. He insisted they required combing daily only if their wool was being collected to sell, something he didn't do, and they were no trouble if you were interested in breeding, *really* interested, he emphasized. 'You mean in the money you get for selling them,' his mother added mischievously.

We all made our way to the most impressive looking kennels I had ever seen. To call them merely kennels is, I suppose, correct, yet it gives a totally inadequate impression. The housing was built of brick with an enclosed run both spacious and providing unhindered look-out. There were two independent sections, each big enough comfortably to accommodate two dogs, and guaranteeing, as we quickly recognized, a perfect place for whelping.

In one of the sections a puppy with his mother was going berserk with excitement at our approach, and in contrast to Happy at our introduction to her rushed toward us as we entered. It looked superb, as lively as the proverbial cricket, and I couldn't help but wonder why this one alone was still unsold. The farmer must have been telepathic, for he straightaway mentioned that all the other puppies were bitches, and spoken for almost before they were conceived, let alone born. 'We have a permanent waiting list,' he smiled. 'But this one,' he picked up the puppy jumping at his legs, 'was the only one not a bitch, and, in my opinion, the best of the bunch.'

He handed it to me. It felt solid, weighty, far more than Happy at a comparable age. 'I'm told you have a bitch,' he chuckled. 'All in good time you'll be able to mate her with this one. I don't suppose you want her to whelp before she's two. At least.'

By now, angora rabbits forgotten for the time being, the puppy was being smothered by the children, he revelling in the fussing no less than they. And few sights are more appealing, I reckon, than a puppy and children at play. In any case, my wife needed no persuading. Taking it for granted we were having the puppy, even before the price was mentioned, she suggested to the children that they find out what Happy thought of the newcomer.

As they disappeared triumphantly to the car, I was coming up for air after learning what the farmer expected me to pay, twice as much as for Happy. Ah, yes, argued this deceptively meek looking man, but his puppies were pedigrees!

Now I've never fully understood the meaning of pedigree in sheepdog circles. Some of the best sheepdogs I know have a Heinz's ancestry; a bit of this and that of many varieties. They prove their pedigree solely by the quality of their work with sheep. Once this is established they qualify for registration with the International Sheepdog Society, and henceforth bring forth pups at – judging by my limited experience – inflated prices. Nevertheless the farmer clearly thought he was doing me a favour as he confirmed the price, and I suspected I was doing him one by accepting without argument.

The other surprise apart from the price was the farmer's bewilderment when I asked for a handful of the puppy's bedding. He'd never heard of this means of reassuring a puppy in a strange setting, and left me in no doubt what he thought about it. Not trying to hide his amusement he grabbed a large handful, and I carried the still wholesome smelling hay to the car.

Happy was decidedly cautious or reserved about the new arrival. While the puppy showed uninhibited delight, Happy kept her distance, or tried to, and even growled a futile warning. The outcome was predictable. By the time we reached home, the older dog was exhibiting every sign of being thoroughly disenchanted, not to say jealous; this young pretender was a menace!

And the children didn't help. They maintained their fussing to the unthinking and never intended exclusion of Happy whose consistent response for weeks was to give as wide a berth as possible to this irrepressible competitor for our attention and affection.

With barely a thought we decided the farmhouse kitchen was big enough to accommodate both dogs for sleeping, a box each. From some standpoints a brick kennel like the one to which the puppy was already accustomed would have been preferable, but with no chance of our ever being able to justify the money and time to build one the new member of the family moved in permanently under our roof.

His name chose itself. Unlike Happy's light brown coat with splashes of white on head, chest, and feet, the puppy was black with a distinctive patch on his right eye. So Patch it was, doubly welcomed by me as I recalled the experts' recommendation of a one syllable name for a working dog. For whether we needed a second dog on the farm or not, and I still thought we didn't, I was determined that Patch should earn his keep. Before the year was out, I was to change my mind in more ways than one, for the worst and the best of reasons.

Colour apart, Patch was readily distinguishable from Happy whatever their distance from me. When he arrived, in keeping with all puppies, he carried his tail up, like an incongruous distress signal, but as he grew and eventually left Happy behind in size it stayed up, never a suggestion of coming down. In his early mischievous days with us, I wondered whether this was an indication that, pedigree lineage or not, he wasn't going to fulfil our hopes or rather confident expectations, particularly after Bill Wheel's verdict that good sheepdogs never worked with their tails up. We needn't have worried.

As soon as Patch started to eye the hens and ducks, and he did very quickly, down came his tail and stayed down until he sent the 'quarry' squawking for cover. I've since discovered a deal of controversy in sheepdog circles about the carriage of the tail. Some farmers claim that a high tail indicates a tendency to play – or to fight! – rather than to herd, while others insist that a dog that never raises its tail lacks courage and is inclined to being morose. My experience was that Patch, tail more often than not aloft, was no less keen to work than Happy, and positively no less courageous. In other words, the carriage of a sheepdog's tail indicates nothing of importance, it seems to me.

But I'm running ahead of the story. For the first weeks Patch showed little inclination to go outside; perhaps the kitchen with its glowing Rayburn was too snug and warm. As with Happy we placed a piece of newspaper near his box, and accustomed him to use the cat flap, hardly any trouble at all. But once he grew too big he faced an obstacle virtually unknown to Happy at a comparable stage in her training. A closed kitchen door.

I've mentioned before that in the summer our kitchen door is rarely closed day and night, offering constant opportunity for nipping outside. With Patch, joining us in the middle of winter, and soon with snow on the ground, we had to take care to make regular opportunities. Not only so, but we needed to stay with him until he'd done the necessary, otherwise his understandable dislike of the cold caused him to sit whining at the door, his need to relieve himself forgotten, forgotten, that is, until almost immediately after his return. No use sticking him outside, ourselves staying in the warm, and expecting him conveniently to commence his whining only after obliging. Fortunately he learned quickly, not least the connection between his speedy co-operation and our united return indoors.

We, on the other hand, were not so quick on the uptake when it came to his involvement with the mystery of the missing kittens. A fortnight or so after their birth they disappeared, evoking a family crisis, and we found them hidden – no other word will do – all over the place – in our bedroom, behind the settee, among logs in the fireside basket, under a chair, behind a curtain, inside the airing cupboard.

For days we assumed their mother was inexplicably

responsible, engaged in this weird form of maternal rejection, but the general quality of the mothering put paid to this mis-information, leaving us to wonder whether such behaviour was an aspect of kitten training we knew nothing about. Once or twice daily we returned the scattered brood to their place of birth, further baffled that they like their mother seemed so unconcerned about the total situation.

The mystery was solved as family and guests, sharing a birthday dinner, paused for second breath before tackling what we thought would be the highlight of the meal, a Black Forest cherry cake with lashings of home-made cream. In walked Patch with an uncomplaining kitten dangling from his mouth. Indifferent to the cries of the children, he gently placed it behind the settee before gingerly disappearing and – like a conjuror repeating a clever trick by popular demand – returned with a second, then a third, and so on until all six were widely dispersed in the by now established hiding places. The *game* was relinquished with the greatest reluctance. In fact, I imagine he would have continued much longer but for the happy diversion of his playfully annoying Happy on a growing scale.

She herself appeared to have her mind on higher things! We worked the trial course about twice a week, but most of our time was spent on winter jobs I certainly loved to hate, guaranteed to cast a shadow over the sunniest disposition. Happy seemed to share my view about hedging and ditching, for increasingly on such occasions she made the point that we weren't as inseparable as I'd fondly imagined.

Unfailingly she joined me as I left the farmhouse, made no attempt to move far as I attended to the animals, and eagerly walked to heel as I plodded to the scene of the day's masochism, but once it became obvious there was to be no reprieve she took to disappearing to the barn in the farmyard, presumably seeking warmth or something better to do.

Ditching – in my experience far worse than hedging – consists of clearing the accumulation of leaves and other deposits of nature's bounty. In theory it is tackled regularly, but I don't know a farm where it is. The usual practice is to leave such a chore until time permits which of course it never does until something like flooding compels action. By the look of things our predecessor had bothered with neither hedging nor ditching for years, the result being that when necessity was laid upon me progress was exceedingly slow.

The one big compensation, for me especially as a newcomer to the countryside, was the opportunity for hours on end to become part of the lonely lovely surroundings, with the chance during breathers simply to look and listen. From this standpoint Happy's disappearance to the barn encouraged the presence of other creatures near at hand, sometimes almost under my nose.

During one break I heard what sounded like a whimper, then a stifled squeal. I stared, hardly daring to breathe – a rabbit confronted by a stoat. For an eternity of seconds neither creature moved; then – flash, it was all over. Only at this point did the stoat, freed of its predator preoccupation, become aware of my presence, and naturally I expected it to scarper, its hunger eclipsed by its instinct for survival. But not on your life.

The stoat was afraid all right, no doubt about that, but before scurrying to safety it dragged its kill, four or five times its own size, deeper into the hedgerow, for attention later. At the time, needless to say, I wasn't sure whether the killer was a stoat or a weasel, and wouldn't swear to it now, though a few days later Bill Wheel tried to put me wise.

The weasel, he rolled off the information, not attempting to hide his contempt for my ignorance, was the smallest of British carnivores, never more than nine inches; whereas the stoat – 'inquisitive little blighter' Bill claimed, often seen standing on its hind legs – was three to four inches longer.

Perhaps significantly my witnessing the kill, far from shocking me, had gripped me with astonishment or wonder. When we first moved to the country, I was without realizing it a sentimentalist about animals both domestic and otherwise, thinking of them as two- or four-legged humans capable of our reasoning, feelings, imagination, anxieties and susceptibilities; extensions of ourselves and *our* emotional needs rather than creatures in their own right, with identities, capacities and needs of their own. It wasn't too long before I recognized that my kindly motivation wasn't always helpful!

Much of what I first saw as cruel and to be prevented if possible by human intervention I now accept as nature's way of controlling, selecting and separating the quick from the dead – the rightful survival of the fittest, essential if hereditary weaknesses are to be eliminated. My conversion wasn't easy, especially in the twilight of myxomatosis! To see its effect on multitudes of living corpses wasn't only an affront to common decency but a big question mark against the ability of the rabbit to survive at all.

One of my neighbours who wouldn't shed a tear if rabbits disappeared off the face of the earth – at least *his* bit of it – drew the line at myxomatosis. Yet these highly vulnerable creatures have proved tougher than the loathsome disease, developing an immunity which reduces its ravishes to near impotence. Virtually any time I glance through an upstairs window in the farmhouse I see them feeding or playfully chasing each other. And as I become part of the landscape with the hedging and ditching some of them seem tame to the point of cheekiness.

As a city dweller dreaming of getting away from it all, I thought of our isolated farm as not only desirable but essential for the peace and quiet we sought. It never crossed our minds there might be snags, like getting snow bound. Mind you, it was rather like living in fairyland.

The morning after it started snowing the drifts were about a foot, and deepening fast, but inconvenience was minimal. In the field nearest the farmhouse the children pelted each other with snowballs, and built a snowman a mile high, reflecting in their enjoyment Happy's excitement at her new experience. She sniffed the snow, rolled in it, ran barking from one child to another as the snowballs flew, and didn't appear to mind when she became a target.

Patch didn't take to the mysterious substance falling from the sky at all. Each time he ventured beyond the kitchen door to relieve himself he barely gave himself time before scampering back to his box by the Rayburn. And the third morning he didn't have much option. We were well and truly snow bound.

I disappeared to the farmyard to get the tractor and hitched on the trailer. The children, wrapped up extra warm, and beside themselves with anticipation climbed aboard. We ploughed our way through drifts sometimes too formidable for my comfort, while the children, bouncing all over the place and constantly urging me to go faster, squealed with delight. Once off the farm track the going was much easier. We turned right at the T-junction opposite the village pub, stopped to pick up a couple of children warily making their way to school on foot, and pulled up outside the school gate as the church clock was striking nine. A notice informed us that the place was closed for the day; inadequate heating!

At the village post office I collected our own mail and that of a couple of neighbours at farms on our way home, and eventually arrived back in our own farmyard to find my wife feeding the hens and ducks, with the news the tap in the cowshed was frozen. Despite these Siberian conditions the children insisted this was the best part of living in the country – fields of snow inches thick offering endless fun, perfect setting for a pitched battle involving every child in the village. My only concession was to promise, school open or not, another tractor ride in the morning.

Of more immediate concern were the sheep. As the weather deteriorated we decided to house them in the Tyler barn, but first, I soon discovered, we had to find them, for three were missing. One, it transpired, was some distance from the other two, but this appeared to present no problem to Happy's internal radar. Hardly hesitating, she pin-pointed each of them which seemed none the worse for their buried experience. She also made little of the difficulties of working the flock, though even the normally truculent leader, a three-lamb ewe, appeared anxious to co-operate in seeking the protection of the barn.

Bill Wheel didn't share my enthusiasm when I told him of this new aspect of Happy's abilities. He admitted that not all sheepdogs were efficient at finding snow-bound sheep, but made me wonder whether he was pulling my leg by telling me of a farmer whose excellent working sheepdog was blind; 'couldn't see a bloody thing' Bill said. As long as the wind was blowing in the right direction, the dog knew exactly where the sheep were, and how to keep them under control because of his highly sensitive nose. Remember what my old friend told you, he concluded, never under-estimate a good sheepdog!

The snowing abated, the temperature rose, but the snow itself on many parts of the farm hung about for weeks. The sheep remained in the barn, and the children, red noses and aching fingers, continued their joy rides on the tractor and trailer. They were the envy of their friends some of whom waited at the T-junction gleefully to scramble aboard at every opportunity.

Happy too didn't stop revelling in the snow, and appeared not to feel the cold. Unlike Patch, still content to stay indoors, she followed me to early morning milking, characteristically quietly waited as I saw to the other animals, and was never less than eager to accompany me whenever I left the farmhouse. The weather being what it was, most of my jobs were indoors, which meant that the dog and I were again virtually inseparable from morning till night.

What we both missed was time on the novice trials course, for about a month, but fortunately, when the snow started to go, one of the first places to clear itself was the meadow. We lost no further time in getting back to training.

Happy was still consistently better with her approach from the left – Come bye – than the right – Away to me – so naturally, if either approach was possible, I chose the former. And on the trials course, more often than not, the five sheep were co-operative, at least from this standpoint. They settled at the far end of the meadow to make my preferred approach not only possible but the better option.

Happy rarely had trouble with the gather, her semi-circular run to get behind the sheep, and likewise with the lift, her point of contact with them as she started to push them forward, but from then on anything seemed likely to go wrong, and often reduced me, never mind the dog, to a bag of nerves. Remember, I'm thinking of marks possibly lost on a trials course, not of what would be perfectly acceptable for a working dog on a farm. Mistakes made then could be quickly rectified, with little inconvenience – well, most of the time! – but every single error during trials meant that many fewer marks.

For instance, Happy's routine herding caused me little trouble; the only thing we occasionally lost was time. She pushed on the flock from A to B, and woe betide any sheep stupid enough to attract attention to itself. On the trials course, the fetch – the distance from the lift to the handler – was something else. She usually eventually managed to get them through the gates all right, but too often only after they'd wandered or been scattered off course, making their approach to the gates more like a shepherd's crook than the straight line I wanted. Worse, after a couple of good gathers she would have the sheep scarpering in all directions at once, and help one or two on their way with a nip. The judges, I recognized, would hardly approve of that!

I'm sure that half the trouble was my own temperament. Despite the near complete privacy of the meadow I behaved as though a crowd were already witnessing – enjoying – my every mistake, laughing their heads off as Happy's enthusiasm took both her and the sheep out of my control. I didn't need Bill to tell me that my apprehension was communicating itself to the dog, and making us both progressively a bundle of nerves.

At one stage, to be honest, I almost decided to forget

novice sheepdog trials, but to do so now, I kept telling myself, would be a greater defeat than any awaiting me on the day itself. More persuasive was the undoubted benefit of all this extra training, an improvement illustrated almost daily in routine activity on the farm. Happy's general efficiency made everything so much easier and, I might add, pleasurable. If ever I needed to separate one or two particular sheep from the flock, for foot inspection or whatever, it was no longer necessary to drive the lot through the separating race and spend ages picking off the ones causing concern. I simply used Happy's sharpened skills to come in when I called and complete the required penning. It wasn't all plain sailing, of course, but the improvement was out of this world.

So we persevered, Happy and I, until I certainly knew the improvised trials course like the back of my hand, and slowly began to believe the whole enterprise wasn't so impossible after all.

A few days later I looked out of the kitchen window, and noticed a single sheep lying in a far corner of the field. Just one. The rest of the flock were grazing in the distance. Why? Well, when a sheep is about to lamb it looks for a quiet corner on its own. A bit of peace and privacy. Then it paws the ground, turns in its own length, paws a bit more, lies down, gets up, and eventually settles to bring forth.

Yes, but this was February, almost the middle of winter. Whoever heard of a lamb being born in the open at this time of the year? More to the point, tupping began on bonfire night with the first lambs not due before April 1st. For a lamb to be born now, conception would have needed to have taken place when the rams were definitely separated from the tegs and ewes. Nevertheless, what was this solitary sheep doing in a far corner?

I strolled across with Happy, but was confounded by the evidence of my own eyes long before I arrived. The lamb, clearly visible, was already suckling. A virgin birth!

Now you can imagine that one of the joys of our sort of farming is the element not only of surprise but unpredictability. Plan as carefully as you like, cater for every contingency, there's usually something totally unexpected to enliven the day. Even so, this really was ridiculous. A lamb with icicles dripping from its nose! I stared at it unbelievingly, and sought revelation.

At which moment a vision of one of our rams beckoned. And I couldn't help laughing out loud. Weeks before tupping, increasingly frisky with the sap rising at every whiff of the flock, he'd broken out, I remembered, to the nearest sheep available, at the time the flock next door. But clearly en route to our neighbour's lovelies he'd found a degree of fulfilment nearer home.

Next morning the phone rang to tell us our neighbour too had an unexpected lamb! Beyond argument the ram's impatience had been less frustrated than we'd imagined. How many more, I wondered? Both lambs, it must be said, were beauties. I brought ours and its mother into an improvised pen in the cowshed, snug, free from draughts, all mod cons laid on for maximum comfort in the circumstances. And both ewe and he did very nicely. As a matter of fact, despite the snow still hanging about on various parts of the farm, I was able to release the pair to pasture, confident the lamb was already sturdy enough to cope with the elements.

This happy interlude should help to correct the possible impression that too much of our time, Happy's and mine, was spent on the trials course in the meadow. The reality was that as lambing proper approached we were able to spend less and less time there, though this was particularly compensated for, in terms of the development of Happy's basic skills, by increased routine activity with the entire flock. For instance, six weeks before April 1st it became necessary to supplement the sheep's daily feed with their favourite indulgence – nutty concentrates guaranteed to contain all the vitamins required for a perfectly balanced diet.

As you should know by now, sheep tell the time by their stomachs. Feed them, as we did, in the region of nine o'clock every morning, and the queue started to form at least ten minutes early at the nearest gate to our approach from the farmyard in the tractor. The bleating and baaing before we arrived was unbelievable. And their individual determination to be first at the feeding troughs as the nuts were poured in presented problems. Ask my wife!

The second morning of this supplementary feeding she volunteered to officiate, leaving me free to attend to Fred the cat lover who'd arrived to help me with a particularly heavy piece of ditching. While we made for the far field, Happy walking to heel, she climbed into the tractor, manoeuvred through the farmyard gate, and revved through the mud. We heard the bedlam of welcome long before she reached the sheep, and vaguely noticed her having a spot of bother persuading them to stand back from the gate to let her through. What finally alerted us that all was far from well was the amplification of the noise.

We gazed across, and quite honestly fell about. In the middle of the marauders was a lone figure struggling like mad to get in. Or out. It was impossible to be sure. The sheep rushed to get at the bag. She held on like grim death, wanting nothing more than to empty its contents into the trough but prevented from doing so by their frantic efforts to help her. Fred nearly did himself a mischief laughing. I too saw nothing but the funny side, until the battling figure suddenly disappeared among the rampaging horde, knocked flying, still gallantly hanging on to her bag of nuts. By the time I breathlessly arrived they were dribbling out of a bursting bottom, while my wife's clothes, like her hands and face, bore evidence of how much sheep eat, given the chance.

Happy soon cleared them away from the trough, but immediately the nuts hit the bottom the entire flock, dog or no dog, swarmed in, again trying to fit their pint of greed into a half-pint of space. You wouldn't believe sheep were capable of such aggression among themselves. Once the second and third troughs were filled congestion eased, though it has to be said that sheep are sometimes so stupid that the majority continued to battle at trough number one until slowly slowly the penny dropped.

Fred was still chuckling when I returned, characteristically without reducing his capacity for work. One of the joys of labouring with Fred, whatever the job, was the way he departmentalized life. When he worked he worked; when he talked he talked; never in my experience did the two overlap. He kept at any, even back breaking, assignment in near total silence, his application always free of haste. As far as most jobs on the land are concerned I know of no one faster or more thorough. Yet, as I say, he never hurried.

The one point at which Fred's general know-how is comprehensively deficient is when he talks about sheep-dogs. He seems dedicated to contradicting the experts. The first time he saw Patch romping with Happy in the farmyard, he confidently informed me that the younger dog would learn all he needed to know simply by working with the older. 'Tie 'em together,' he advised, 'he'll soon pick up the right ideas.'

Fred isn't the only one! Even W. H. Hudson, in his acknowledged classic 'A Shepherd's Life', had this to say about a young sheepdog: 'Another thing. He must be made to work with an old sheepdog, for though he has the impulse to fly about and do something, he does not know what to do and does not understand his master's gestures and commands. He must have an object lesson, he must see the motion and hear the word and mark how the old dog flies to this or that point and what he does. The word of command or the gesture thus becomes associated in his mind with a particular action on his part. But he must not be given too many object lessons or he will lose more than he will gain – a something which might almost be described as a sense of individual responsibility. That is to say, responsibility to the human master who delegates his power to him. Instead of taking his power directly from the man he takes it from the dog, and this becomes a fixed habit so quickly that many shepherds say that if you give more than from three to six lessons of this kind to a young dog you will spoil him. He will need the mastership of the other dog, and will therefore always be at a loss and work in an uncertain way.'

In summing up this reputed shepherding practice, Mr Hudson does, however, sound a note of caution: 'A timid or unwilling young dog is often coupled with the old dog two or three times, but this method has its dangers too, as it may be too much for the young dog's strength, and give him that *broken heart* from which he will never recover; he will never be a good sheepdog.'

Fortunately I'd already picked up from what was by

now my sheepdog training bible – John Holmes's 'The Farmer's Dog' – that dogs should work together, but never be tied together, only *after* each had been thoroughly grounded in basic skills. I mentioned this to Fred whose look of disbelief confirmed his agreement with Hudson.

Whatever his opinion about sheepdogs, and my opinion about his opinion, we were agreed that Patch, still content merely to make the life of the hens and ducks less than tranquil, looked a good 'un. It's hard to put into words exactly the reason for such optimism, but it never occurred to me to doubt, most of all after I'd seen both Patch's parents in action.

I'd gone across to collect two angora rabbits, [outcome, incidentally, of a growing teenage friendship that appeared to have more than rabbits as its first interest] and arrived as the flock was to be put through the footrot bath. The two dogs shot off in opposite semi-circular directions, arrived simultaneously for the lift, and worked together with barely a command. If Patch proved to be half as competent I'd have no complaints.

More impressive still was how one of the dogs, the bitch, dealt with an awkward ewe, the leader, I gathered, of the flock, with a well deserved reputation for making trouble. As they neared the penned area giving access to the walk-through bath, she turned defiantly to face the dog, not a flicker of hesitation, and charged. When the dog didn't budge, the ewe stepped back and charged again. And again. This third time, the dog still immovable and in fact inching forward, the ewe's fighting spirit collapsed and meekly she fell into line. It all sounds so commonplace, but in like circumstances I'd seen enough experienced dogs either slightly back off or stand indecisively not to appreciate the degree of courage required.

I'd also seen a tough old ewe actually take on a young dog and not back off, repeatedly charging until the dog not the ewe had done a bunk. The farmer, I wasn't a bit surprised to learn, had subsequently sold the young pretender to city people who'd always wanted a sheepdog!

Anyhow, reassured about Patch's pedigree in the only way I cared about, I packed the rabbits in the car, and gratefully accepted an invitation to join the farmer and his wife for a quick coffee in the farmhouse. Did I say *quick*? More than an hour later I ran to the car, the three of us cursing ourselves for not having noticed the time. The trouble was, though certainly I'm not complaining, I got them talking about their farming background, and in the light of their stranger than fiction story found it impossible not to go on asking questions.

Surprise number one – both had been born and brought up in London. Yet he inexplicably, for as long as he could remember, had wanted to be a farmer, absolutely obsessed with the idea. His parents didn't approve, and hoped he'd grow out of it. None of their forbears were farmers or anything remotely like. On the contrary they'd lived in the city for generations, and he was expected, finally coerced, to do the same.

Then how, I wondered, did he manage to break free? His matter of fact answer left me dumbfounded. Poker faced, clearly not aware he was saying anything unusual, he said he took a correspondence course in pig farming! Forget that there wasn't a pig in sight on his present farm, this pragmatic man's casual reply left, as Frankie Howerd would say, my flabber gasted. I couldn't believe it. 'I tell you,' he read my astonishment, 'I did a correspondence course in pig farming.'

His wife laughed out loud at my uncertainty whether or not he was pulling my leg. 'It's true,' she assured me, taking up the story. Having established himself as a highly successful commercial artist, he saved like a miser, and kept his ear to the ground for information about any small holding in the country, even a farm, if the price was right. These were the days, she reminded me, before the price of land rocketed beyond the pocket of ordinary people.

Well, eventually he found a suitable property, and managed with what little money he had left to buy a few pigs, meanwhile earning his living as a factory night watchman in a nearby town. After a few weeks of this agony, deciding he'd rather starve than stay in the job, and determined not to go back to his commercial art inevitably centred in London, he found himself a part-time job with a pig farmer up the road.

She paused, her eyes dancing with affection as she turned to her husband. This was, she went on, before we met, but the way he still talks about those pigs, his own and the farmer's, you'd think they were his brothers and sisters. He shuffled uneasily, for countrymen – and he looked one to his finger tips – can't abide townee senti-mentality about animals, domesticated or wild. Yet almost defiantly he addressed his wife: 'I loved those pigs. What's so funny about that?' There was amusement in his voice, but no mistaking his seriousness. Little more was said along these lines, but I gathered that the issue was something of a sore point between them. And in the light of what she told me next I could understand why.

He worked hard, all the hours of day and night, his pigs farrowed regularly, and by keeping his best stock for breeding he outgrew the farmer for whom he initially worked, and within seven years was able to buy him up, lock, stock and barrel. Her husband sipped his coffee, a wicked or rather teasing look in his eyes. It wasn't long after this, she continued, that we met. I was a ward sister, and he came into hospital for one of those unmentionable operations.

Their laughter now mingled as each tried to take up the story. He wasn't a good patient, she said, we couldn't wait to see the back of him. But the night before he was due for discharge, not a hint of a warning, he asked me to marry him. Just like that, out of the blue. Nonsense! he gently mocked; you'd been softening me up from the first day. And what did you say – remember? I told you, she replied, what I kept telling you – you could have either me or the pigs, not both; and it was only after a lot of thought you condescended to tell me I was preferable to the pigs!

There followed a good deal of happy banter, given and received with obvious affection, but this whole question of pigs was, as I say, evidently a sore point between them. 'I can't abide the smell of pigs,' she said, 'despite my husband telling me they don't smell.'

In the circumstances I decided to stay neutral. Even so, I felt for the pigs, never mind the ex-pig farmer who, escorting me to the car, confessed he'd never regretted moving over to sheep. 'Another correspondence course?' I asked facetiously. The noisy emptiness of his laughter advised me not to wait for an answer, but to turn the conversation back to the working skills of Patch's parents.

How Patch himself would square up we had no means of knowing. All the signs looked good, but we knew that the tendency – merely the *tendency* – to back off in danger sometimes afflicted the most promising sheepdogs. Patch's time would come. Until then we could only hope.

Happy was nothing if not courageous, proved time and again, but unfortunately the same couldn't always be said for her intelligence. Perhaps I'm being too hard, but at times her capacity to infuriate seemed at least proportionate to her ability at other times to please. We'd go for as long as a fortnight or three weeks with her giving every satisfaction, and then conspicuously one after another she'd have a series of off days. Why, for instance, did she not always understand practised commands, looking at me as though utterly bewildered, or, surely understanding, proceed to do the opposite, or, using her own initiative, create little but chaos?

It was this latter failing that caused me most trouble and disappointment. For on her good days she could be depended upon both to compensate for any oversight on my part and resolve unexpected difficulties. In fact, sometimes I found myself talking out loud to her about all sorts of problems as though she could understand every word and come up with the answers. Whose to wonder? when, you remember, she found the prostrate sheep or uninvited sprang into the pen to preoccupy the rams as I dived for their hocks or pushed the flock through the separating race with such efficiency that I called to her, 'Is that the lot?'! Superb sheepdog.

But she didn't do much compensating for anything when her impetuosity had scattered the sheep, apart from nipping a few backsides. This still bothered me a lot, bearing in mind the sheepdog trials, but Bill Wheel continued to argue that a good working sheepdog needed to nip any tough old ewe to teach it who was boss. Those trials judges are 'silly buggers', all wind and theory and incapable of recognizing a good farm dog when they see one. 'A nip ain't a bite,' he repeated another of his favourite sayings.

Truth to tell, most sheepdog handlers I met shared Bill's idea about nipping, giving this as one reason why they couldn't be bothered with trials. A dog, they argued, might lose every point possible according to a trials judge's marking, but still be a first class working dog where it mattered most – on the farm. They are right, no doubt, but this doesn't alter the fact that the best trials dogs are almost invariably also the best farm dogs.

What finally convinced me that I was largely to blame for the majority, if not all, of Happy's off days happened shortly before lambing got underway. Almost before it started it had been one of those days! I'd woken early, dropped off to sleep again, been late for milking to be greeted not only by two over-loaded housecows but the noisy indignation of the calves protesting about late breakfast, the car wouldn't start to get the children to school on time, and – unbelievably – the Rayburn went out. By the time we were back to some degree of normality, half the morning had gone and I still had to tackle the one weekly chore I disliked more than anything.

You doubtless know quite a lot about mucking *in*, those occasions when everybody lends a hand, but mucking *out* is something else, a lonely encounter if you live on a one-man farm where all the animals share the same ambition to provide more fertilizer than you know what to do with, and always in the wrong place.

What added to the problem at this particular time was our preparation for lambing. We decided to bring the flock under cover each night to simplify regular inspections and also facilitate speedier remedies in emergencies. A wise precaution! But one consequence, massively illustrated already by our previous accommodation of the sheep under cover – during the worst of the snow – was a mountain of shit in the barn requiring urgent removal. What with this, and the calves still housed until milder

110

weather, my hands were, to say the least, full to overflowing.

Knackered and stinking to high heaven, I eventually finished, rushed indoors for a belated lunch, and burping heavily stumbled from the farmhouse to start another filthy job – dagging, euphemism for arse trimming, short back and sides at the vulva, essential for hygienic lambing deliveries.

Things didn't improve. The sheep were bloody minded, Happy belied her name, as fed up with the whole weary business as I, my back was killing me, the dung-saturated wool seemed adhesive, and, as though this wasn't enough, the car again refused to start for my wife to collect the children from school.

One by obstinate one I resumed picking off the sheep, held them between my legs, and clipped judiciously in the appropriate area, an exercise wholly at variance with the romantic idea beloved by non-sheep farmers. It wasn't the polluted backsides themselves that bothered me, but somehow every little inconvenience like my dropping the clippers or a sheep deciding to defecate as I did the dagging irritated me out of all proportion.

Happy remained subdued long after the sheep were settled for the night, and even when, realizing I was responsible, I called her to me for a cuddle, her tail stayed firmly between her legs. The fussing appeared to make her less sure still, for during the rest of that day her eyes never lost their anxiety.

Lambing started in the middle of the night. Our experienced neighbours had assured us that most lambs were born during the day, and doubtless this is the case. All I can say is that our lambs too often proved to have a pronounced inclination to reveal themselves as we waited to go to bed. Our very first lamb was a case in point. I went to give the flock a final inspection, flashed my torch round the barn, and spotted a ewe in labour. More correctly she was showing all the signs of labour – turning in her own length, lying down, getting up, pawing the straw, turning again, and finally settling. The birth was clearly imminent.

Having been told often enough that the best policy with a ewe in labour, in fact, with any animal in labour, was to leave her undisturbed to get on with it, I set the alarm for four hours, and wearily climbed the stairs. The subsequent inspection vindicated my confidence, for there in the straw were twins, one of them already searching for a teat. Despite the hour – I wouldn't bother to this degree now! – I moved the trio to one of our makeshift pens in the cowshed, and returned to bed. Incidentally, assuming the lambs were born after midnight, they arrived spot on April 1st!

Soon after first light I let the rest of the flock out to pasture in a field within easy sight of the farmhouse. It was simple to get them there without the help of Happy or anyone else. All I needed to do was pour the concentrates into the troughs in the field, remove the hurdle at the barn door, and stand back sharpish. The ensuing stampede was no place for the unwary.

At about mid-morning my wife noticed a ewe showing all the usual lambing signs. An hour later she wondered why progress, if any at all, was so slow. Another three hours passed; labour was clearly underway, but the stalemate continued. As I approached for a closer look the ewe or more correctly teg (a sheep never having lambed before) made not the slightest attempt to move.

Careful neither to waste a moment nor to hurry, I lubricated my hand and arm with soap flakes, and felt my

112

way along the vagina into the womb. No doubt about the holdup – the lamb was coming head first, making birth impossible. Fortunately it wasn't difficult to pull first one leg, then the other forward, and – harmonizing with the sheep's strains – ease the lamb down the birth passage. It fell to the straw apparently more dead than alive, but within minutes was struggling to its feet searching for a teat.

Lambs soon seemed to be everywhere, a constant procession into the makeshift pens in the cowshed for a twenty-four-hour check-up with their mums. Getting the family units into the pens initially proved less than straightforward, until we realized the secret was simultaneously to keep the new born at the mother's eye level and within easy smelling distance, otherwise she rushed back to the place of birth in frantic search of the lamb.

Having got them there and happily settled, another early job was to mark sheep and offspring with the same number, mainly for easier identification and to indicate order of birth. We quickly became practised at this too, though admittedly some of the numbers on ewes determined to be unco-operative occasionally took a bit of deciphering.

We were also always glad to get behind us the docking of tails and the castration of male lambs. Usually my wife held the lambs as I used a special instrument so simple to operate to fit a rubber band round the top of the tail, and another round the scrotum. It might sound cruel, but in fact the lambs didn't appear to notice either at the time or subsequently. And after a fortnight or so, the supply of blood cut off, both tail and scrotum withered away.

What happened finally in our post-lambing pens before the family units were released to specially reserved pasture amused some of our neighbours and delighted the children. Despite the leg-pulling and laughter, my wife and I remain convinced our precaution paid off. In any case, if once you'd come across a lamb lying in a field either dead or dying you feel inclined to adopt what looks to some people like extreme measures.

We picked out the weaker lambs, and fitted a plastic coat for protection from wind and rain. I readily concede it looked hilarious, even ridiculous, but nothing will persuade us it didn't help to keep our mortality rate remarkably low. Yes, but we too still couldn't help but see the funny side every time the lambs, each numbered, plastic coats resembling saddles, raced from one part of the field to another, like Derby runners. And if after a couple of weeks or so the coats, torn, twisted, falling off, brought a comic element into our shepherding, who cared if their purpose was already fulfilled!

It didn't always work, of course. I remember finding a lamb, born sickly but apparently no longer in danger, lying dead, its eyes picked out doubtless by crows. Not more than a couple of hours before I'd watched it frisking with the others, watched it with great satisfaction, knowing how nearly it had been still-born.

Irrationally cursing the marauders for obeying nothing more than their own instinctive viciousness I picked up the lamb and carried it to the farm workshop to await disposal. It looked pathetic, adding to my guilt as well as my disappointment, for the thought haunted me – could I have done more to protect it? Never mind a plastic coat, should I have kept it indoors with the mother for longer than the three days I had thought adequate?

A noise in the farmyard indicated the arrival of a neighbour, most unusual for him, smiling all over his face, a lamb in each hand. Would I, he asked, like a couple of sock lambs? For FREE! Now I was aware that

114

farmers with sizeable flocks frequently sold sock lambs cheaply, happy to see the back of such time-consuming orphans requiring bottle feeding every four hours, initially day and night, but to be offered two for nothing! However, I must be honest and admit they looked barely more alive than the corpse in the workshop.

'I've only one pair of hands,' my neighbour smiled at my surprise that he wanted nothing for them and off he went.

I too didn't hang about. Sharpening my shepherd's knife, I skinned the dead lamb, careful to remove the tiny jacket in one piece. It proved an easier job than I'd feared. Then Happy and I nipped to the pasture to pick off the bereaved ewe. She appeared wholly unconcerned about her missing lamb, illustrating what never ceased to astonish me – the speed with which animals recover in such situations. No doubting their strong maternal instinct, but to pine for their dead seems outside their capacity.

Happy excelled herself. Once the ewe was identified, the dog took her through two gates and into the cowshed, waiting for me to complete the penning. I slipped the hurdle back into position, and turned to the smaller of the sock lambs. It lay on the straw, too weakly to struggle as I fitted the skin. Fitted? It looked like a badly packed parcel.

Nevertheless, conscious that the smell of the skin, not its appearance, might do the trick, I placed the orphan in the pen, and hoped. The ewe sniffed, turned away, suspicious, sniffed again, and butted the lamb aside. I tried again, this time holding the ewe steady as I plugged the lamb on to a teat, but at the first opportunity the ewe cocked her leg in dismissal, sending the tiny orphan flying.

The lamb once more tried to suckle, with similar results. But this time the ewe's positive rejection was tempered by a first sign of real doubt. She sniffed repeatedly, turned away in disbelief, sniffed a bit more, her eyes puzzled, perhaps tender? These manoeuvrings continued for ten minutes or so, the balance of the ewe's indecision always finally tipped against acceptance.

I was beginning to wonder about this traditional shepherding ruse, when in walked Bill Wheel with the news his second Jersey had calved – another lovely heifer. Steadily he stared at the lamb, its disguise by now decidedly out of joint, and then at me, his face alive with mockery. 'Silly bugger,' he muttered his favourite endearment, 'what're you playing at fancy dress parades for?' Not waiting for an answer he grabbed the ewe and held it steady as the lamb suckled.

Having tried this tactic myself, I waited with a degree of smugness for him to let go. Bill held on, still encouraging the lamb to suckle, and asked me to place Happy inside the pen no more than three strides from the ewe. She watched the operation with obvious anxiety, not for a moment taking her eyes off the dog.

'This should do the trick,' Bill whispered, explaining that the ewe's maternal feelings for the lamb would be quickened by her instinctive concern to defend it from the dog.

It worked. True, it took time; the ewe, normally timid even in the distant presence of Happy, unhesitatingly faced the dog and looked prepared to fight, while Happy herself sat benignly, a picture of no nonsense vigilance, and by the end of the afternoon ewe and lamb were bonded inseparably.

Privately I still wondered to what extent the skin of the dead lamb had contributed to this outcome, but our next

116

adoption without a skin vindicated Bill's method; and so it continues, but not, I must add, with guaranteed success.

I came across one ewe, with a lamb's head, no sign of the feet, peering from her backside. Normally this wouldn't cause any trouble – the head would be pushed back into the womb, the legs pulled forward, and the birth take place. But on this one occasion I stared at the head in astonishment.

It was twice the normal size, grotesque in the extreme, and – to be frank – rather unnerving; frightening. The eyes bulged like organ stops, massively proclaiming the lamb was dead, and equally hauntingly the whole face was black. Good job my sentimentality about animals was fading, for this situation was clearly no place for the squeamish.

My dilemma was, of course, that the corpse couldn't leave the birth passage because the feet weren't forward, and I couldn't push it back into the womb to get them forward because of the giant head. Actually, I tried or rather only started to try; within seconds it was obvious I was attempting the impossible. So what to do?

The solution slowly dissolved in my mind like a sucked lozenge, compelling me, incidentally, to recognize that I wasn't so much an ex-townee after all. The lamb would have to be decapitated!

Swallowing hard, my heart thumping, I started to cut. On paper this doubtless sounds straightforward – a bold incision, and the rest follows automatically. Almost. But I was no more a surgeon than an experienced shepherd. To add to the trauma, the ewe wasn't steady, spasmodically lively, in fact, apparently as intent on keeping her lamb in one piece as I was on removing the head.

As it fell to the straw the next problem immediately presented itself. Protruding from the tiny body was the neck bone, capable of tearing the ewe's innards to pieces as I pushed it back into the womb. What wouldn't I have given at that moment for the presence of the vet or even Bill Wheel! But time was of the essence.

Wrapping the palm of my hand round the bone I started to push. Understandably the blood and slime didn't help my grip, but I managed to keep the jagged pieces well covered, and eventually eased the headless corpse into the womb. Whether the ewe realized what I was about I cannot, of course, be sure, but she seemed altogether quieter as though trying to be helpful. Indeed, without such co-operation I doubt whether I would have been able to protect her from the bone as I pulled the legs forward and began the return journey.

During the next few seconds I discovered that the distance from the womb to the vulva was endless. The ewe strained, I pulled on the bone, PULLED, I tell you, but the reluctance of that headless corpse to be born assumed gigantic proportions. The ewe, as I say, was helpful, the lamb's shrunken body the contrast to its massive head, yet for some reason the tiny corpse seemed to be fighting to stay in or near the womb. Grimly I held on to that bone, and longed for delivery!

When finally the bloody mess flopped on to the straw my desperation quickly gave way to sadness and anger. Why did nature play such dirty tricks? It was bad enough to deal with the occasional still-born lamb, but this was somehow indecent, an affront to one's sensibilities. All right, so I am learning not to be sentimental about animals, but on this occasion I had to fight to stem the tears. God's in his heaven, all's *wrong* with the world! just about summed up my feelings.

As for the ewe, she appeared in no time at all to be totally forgetful of or indifferent to the whole experience.

Once inside her post-natal pen, she tucked into her special ration of concentrates, and gave about as much evidence of being bereaved as a bride on her wedding day.

Fortunately I didn't have time to wallow in my own wretchedness. Here was a lambless ewe with overflowing teats. Why was I hanging about? Our by now five sock lambs included one from a set of triplets whose mother didn't have enough milk for all three. In any case, having suckled it normally with the other two, she began increasingly to indicate that this weakest of the three was no longer welcome to join the others. If the poor little feller was to survive at all, he required an alternative source of supply. Bottle feeding I had decided, it had to be.

But possibly not any more! I ran to the barn, scooped him up, and – despite his baaing protests – tenderly placed him beside the bereaved ewe. As I expected, she sniffed, and turned her back. What I didn't expect was the belligerence of her rejection, for once more she turned, and this time butted the lamb to the other side of the pen.

I grabbed the ewe, allowed the lamb to suckle, which he was delighted to do, and called Happy into the pen, confident this would do the trick. The ewe's almost immediate response was, dog or no dog, repeatedly to butt the lamb aside, and finally as far as I could make out try to hoof him clean out of the pen. We tried again. And again. But this ewe could hardly have been less inhibited by Happy as far as her rejection of the lamb was concerned. It didn't take me long to accept that she wasn't going to tolerate him at any price.

A few days before, my wife was telling me of a radio programme in which young mothers talked of their bewilderment and guilt at finding themselves incapable spontaneously of loving their own children; and sheep too, believe me, get caught up in this maternal enigma, not often in my experience, but when they do some of them are capable of unbelievable aggression. So back to the bottle went the rejected triplet; and – after a couple of days to check all was well after such a grim labour – back to pasture went the lambless ewe, once more significantly strictly under Happy's control.

Bottle feeding wasn't all fun, particularly when each lamb demanded preferential attention from unavoidably limited pairs of hands, not all fun, that is, until my wife resolved the whole four-hourly baaing hullabaloo in one moment of inspiration. She punctured the sides of an ordinary bucket, fitted a teat at each hole, and poured in the powdered milk. Instantaneous silence! The hungry orphans helped themselves in unison.

Even the vet was impressed. He called to do a routine blood test on the calves, and smiled approvingly at the bucket. Unfortunately two or three of the young bullocks seemed determined to put the smile on the other side of his face. I'd haltered them with the others in a neat row, all ready and waiting, but they bucked and battled to get at least as much of his blood as he struggled to extract a sample of theirs.

Why our normally well behaved animals invariably let us down in front of visitors we have never understood, unless hopefully it's nothing more than our townee background prompting us to feel embarrassed for largely imaginary reasons. At all events, the vet was laughingly undeterred, and assured us the calves seemed in good condition.

By now lambs seemed to be everywhere. In bunches of twenty or thirty, sometimes more, they raced up the field wild with ecstasy, incapable of containing their supercharged zest. I wouldn't be surprised if the sight of lambs at play originated the saying 'Spring's in the air', for ours constantly took off on all fours and seemed reluctant at times to come down. An old shepherd once told me he kept young in spirit by watching his lambs frolicking. 'I reckon,' he laughed, 'they make me feel half my age.' Certainly I defy anyone to walk through a field of lambs without feeling at least ten years younger. It's their bursting vitality that does it, this and their irrepressible love of life.

Mind you, few sights are more pathetic than lambs caught in a downpour or piercing wind, but even then they're rarely subdued for long. How often have I watched them overcoming the elements with what looked like organized games of joyful confusion – falling over themselves or each other in skipping and dancing, chasing or investigating rabbits which appeared to join in the fun, and – apparently favourite of all – tearing up and down the field like fierce competitors who nevertheless didn't care in the least about coming first or last.

The same, alas, could not be said any more about some of a distant neighbour's lambs. Weeks before lambing actually started she warned me of the menace of foxes. From the wood adjacent to her small holding, they found it simple to prowl on her new born lambs, making off with some while the ewes were still preoccupied with the afterbirth. How she eventually coped with this I discovered for myself one unforgettable night.

Long after the village garage had closed, I ran out of petrol, and had no option but to leg it back to the farm, fortunately a short cut through the woods adjacent to her smallholding. Happy kept close at heel as I groped my way through the trees, cursing myself for being such an idiot about the petrol.

Unexpectedly we came to a boundary, unexpectedly because by my calculations we should have been somewhere near the middle of the woods by now, but such concerns barely crossed my mind as I gazed in charmed bewilderment. I crept nearer, intrigued, baffled, and inexplicably apprehensive. Twinkling lights surrounded the whole of my neighbour's flock, about thirty sheep in all. I felt I'd stumbled across fairyland.

Closer inspection revealed candles in jam jars, each evenly spaced at no more than half a dozen strides. I stood racking my brain for an explanation. None of my vastly experienced farming friends had mentioned anything remotely like this – burning candles in jars around a lambing field – and in all the sheep-and-lambing manuals I'd devoured over the past months there hadn't been one reference.

The rest of the journey home I didn't notice as I pondered the insoluble, and still baffled stepped into the farmhouse immediately to pick up the phone. My neighbour laughed, then expressed amazement. Surely by now I'd heard of this old shepherding practice! And make no mistake, she went on, since adopting it not a single lamb had been taken by foxes.

But the next time I called at her place to buy some honey from her bees, a local luxury, she was less sanguine. Oh, the foxes had remained no problem throughout this year's lambing, undoubtedly deterred by the illuminations, but she wished she could say the same for – MINKS. Pardon? I said. MINKS, she repeated.

Now by one of those peculiarities of timing I'd read in the previous day's Guardian a piece by naturalist William Condry about minks. Rejoicing that the otter was now legally protected, he bemoaned the fact that former otter hunters had taken to hunting another waterside animal, the mink, though they must be fully aware that mink hunting is still a major disturbance to otters. 'So why,' he concluded, 'can't mink hunting also be made illegal?'

'Are you sure minks were the culprits?' I half apologized, Condry in mind. Almost immediately I knew the question was ill advised. To say no more, the animated reply left me in no doubt. How was she so sure? In a word, the carnage. 'Once you've seen the work of the mink,' her venom almost spit in my eye, 'you can't fail to recognize the signs.' She paused to wind herself up. 'I was so angry,' she unnecessarily told me, 'the lambs weren't only newly born. One was taken at two weeks.'

Bill wasn't so easily convinced about the mink. He listened to my tale, agreed the creatures were 'vicious little buggers', but remained highly sceptical about their preying on lambs. Even so, though I haven't yet found it necessary to start collecting jam jars for candles, one thing's for sure – I shall never again react as I did when I thought I spotted a mink during ditching: 'Can't do any harm on the farm,' I yielded to its undoubted visual appeal.

I was, however, increasingly less sure about my attitude toward foxes. Farmers and countrymen generally, it didn't take me long to discover, tend to fall into one of two categories as far as this wily predator is concerned. A friend of mine in the next village, farming in his blood for generations, won't allow foxes to be hunted on his farm under any circumstances. Not that he's partial to foxes above other wild creatures. It's simply that – being an arable farmer – he's never less than enthusiastic to give rabbits as hard a time as possible.

I'm inclined to go along with him for another reason altogether, a joke to Bill and other countrymen I know like him. In a word I *admire* foxes. Not that Bill doesn't, but he also looks upon them as a bloody nuisance, to put it no stronger, when they prey on lambs, something I know nothing about at first hand. And if the pelt of a fox can earn him a bob or two on the side, Bill thinks this reason enough to reach for his home-made snares.

The fox's appeal from my standpoint was, I must admit, substantially reduced when four of our laying hens went missing, with plenty of evidence left behind to indicate a fox. This apart, I'd recently seen one skirting the farm, looking as guilty as hell, but irrationally still felt inclined to give it the benefit of the doubt. Bill's reaction was to call me a silly bugger and accuse me of lingering townee sentimentality. Perhaps he was right.

At the time, in any case, I had another more pressing concern – whether a small sheep farm like ours was ultimately financially viable at all. After another tossing and turning sort of night, this explains why I was up well before first light once more heading for the woods, my favourite place for being alone to think.

Somehow I find the company of trees an antidote to short-sighted worrying, and on this occasion they gently prised my mind away from things I could do nothing about (certainly not immediately, if at all) and focused it on ordering a list of priorities. Sounds elementary, but I didn't and don't find it easy.

I remember envying Bill Wheel's carefree attitude to life; nothing ever seemed to worry him, not for long. He appeared content to live a day at a time, and leave tomorrow to take care of itself. The reason, he once shyly told me, was not so much the outcome of being a countryman all his life but the few days years ago he was in hospital for tests concerning what he increasingly believed was a terminal disease. Made me think, he smiled.

Idly I wandered through the trees, soaking up the peace and beauty all around me. A path took me into that part of the woods where I'd first come across the craftsman making bundles of pales for fencing. I listened for any sound of his presence. Nothing.

Suddenly a movement caught my eye, barely half-a-dozen strides away. I froze on the spot, hardly daring to breathe. Two fox cubs were snarling fun at each other – stalking, pouncing, biting, rolling locked together, play-fully learning the skills of hunting and killing. Was it really possible, the alien thought struck me, that these cuddly creatures were the greedy recipients of pickings from our hens?

I must have stood for two or three minutes before one of them noticed me, and the pair shot down their earth only strides away. Cautiously my eyes searched for the vixen.

There she was, lazily outstretched, basking in the first rays of the sun, a picture of contented motherhood. Slowly she bestirred herself, progressively nervous, mystified, somehow aware her cubs were no longer play-ing. She looked around, spotted me, and was off like a rocket, her cubs apparently forgotten or left to their fate.

Inevitably I recalled the lad I came across on the other side of the farm, a gentle lad known in the village as a budding ornithologist. Between sobs he told me that, climbing a tree and meaning no harm, he'd been attacked by a bird. I explained the tawny owl's concern for her young; if she thought them in danger she'd defend them against any intruder, size and friendly intention notwithstanding.

Unlike this fox! She was off, her maternal instinct overwhelmed by her urge for self-preservation. Or so I concluded at the time. Bill put me right the moment I told him. 'She wasn't deserting her cubs,' he grumbled at my ignorance, 'she was laying a scent away from them in the hope you'd follow. Crafty little bugger,' he added affectionately.

He also strongly made the point that the cubs were so energetic, and likely to get more so, because of their chicken diet! And on the spot he offered to bring in his Jack Russells for a speedy defence of my birds. When I hesitated he eyed me with a little snort of despair.

What finally tipped the scales in favour of drastic action was the premature solving of our fighting cockerel problem. This self-crowned king of the farmyard, too often sentinel against the children's freedom to walk unmolested beyond the farmhouse garden, was undone, he and three more of his harem, undone furthermore by the audacity of a late afternoon raid my wife actually witnessed. Enough was enough.

I still felt wretched, however, when Bill and a friend, notorious locally for his hunting and reputed poaching exploits, arrived with Bill's Jack Russells. Not that either of them, I'm sure, noticed my lingering reluctance. Their assumption understandably was that this latest trouble with a fox had at least made my admiration and respect for the animal less tolerant.

The two men seemed in no hurry. Two or three cups of tea in the farmhouse, and lots of talk in the farmyard before, apparently as an afterthought, they wandered toward the woods, a couple of deep dyed countrymen totally at ease with each other and the business in hand. Actually, Bill's mate looked the part even more than Bill himself. Baler twine just below each kneecap lifted the bottom half of his trousers, revealing fearsome boots reaching three or four inches above his ankles; knotted round his neck was a red, white spotted handkerchief, a size and style I hadn't seen anywhere for years. In truth the only thing missing from this traditional picture of a country bumpkin was a piece of straw in the mouth.

But there, I quickly realized, any resemblance to a simpleton stopped abruptly. This man didn't miss a trick. Nevertheless he straightaway absolutely staggered me by saying he daily commuted from his cottage to a town ten or so miles away, struggled with factory claustrophobia at his semi-skilled job, and lived for the freedom of the week-ends. Why in the world did he do it?

These days, he explained, with a wife and family to support, he couldn't afford to be choosy. Farm wages weren't too bad when he was single; but when the first baby came along he and his wife simply couldn't manage on the money. As a farm worker the only way to earn enough was to put the hours in, seven days a week. He preferred the purgatory of five days at the factory with every week-end free to do as he liked.

I must say, he seemed cheerful enough, and laughter was never far away as we moved toward the woods. You could call him, I suppose, the best example of a country wag, and this capacity for fun was illustrated as he responded to Bill's invitation to tell me about the leg of roasted fox!

It centred upon one of the man's factory workmates, a bragging individual who rubbed them all up the wrong way by insisting that whatever they had done he had done better. A proper little know-all. Finally exasperated, the countryman decided it was time for a bit of purposeful fun.

'Even *you*,' he addressed the man at a crowded table

in the factory canteen, 'haven't enjoyed a luxury we enjoy in the country. Roasted fox!'

The man admitted that this was the case, but, also as expected, said he'd be prepared to taste it, given the chance. Good enough, the countryman played the man along, are you saying if I brought you some you'd eat it? He laughed in disbelief; I bet you wouldn't. The man's bravado was now thoroughly roused. You bring it, he kept repeating, I'll eat it. Anything for a laugh.

So that night the former farm worker went hunting, with a torch, and of course his gun. He skinned the victim in no time, drying the pelt for subsequent sale to a contact in the fur trade, and handed to his mildly protesting wife a leg to roast. No use, he argued with her, taking raw meat to work. The man would take it away and simply claim he'd cooked and eaten it.

Next morning, saying nothing to anyone, he took the less than appetizing result of his wife's handiwork to the factory canteen and brought it out at the customary crowded table. The man's face drained of colour. The peculiar pungent smell added to his obvious reluctance even to touch it. Well, come on, said the countryman, let's see you eat it!

'It's not really fox meat, is it?' appealed the man.

'As fresh as last night's new moon,' said the countryman, 'and roasted to perfection by my wife.'

The poor man was undone, not shame-faced enough to chicken out, too proud not to, surrounded by hooting workmates daring him to funk it after all his loud promises.

He raised the roasted meat to his nose, grimaced, laughed nervously, and – finally convinced there was nothing else for it – sank his teeth. Next moment, to ironic cheers, he bolted for the toilets.

'Teach him a lesson, I shouldn't wonder,' Bill couldn't stop laughing; and thoughtfully suggested that the next time any of our townee friends paid us a visit we too should serve them with this noted country delicacy, and tell them only afterwards what they'd eaten.

In such a happy frame of mind we arrived in the vicinity of the fox earth, but then all larking about ceased, and all necessary conversation was reduced to a whisper. The matter in hand was clearly deadly serious, not least for the dogs which immediately celebrated the prospect by sniffing out the fox's urine and excitedly rolling in it, apparently a favourite indulgence. Within seconds they were stinking to high heaven. To put it no stronger.

Satisfied by the dogs' activity at the earth's entrance that the quarry was at home, the two experts fitted a net there, slipped the smallest dog under, and pegged the bottom firm. Bill and his mate cocked their ears, and consulted each other in sign language. Briefly there was silence from the underworld, then growing yapping, growling, snarling.

Bill's mate started digging. Another spadeful. Another. And there was the fox, its teeth buried in the dog's nose. The canine hunter rather than the hunted seemed helpless. It struggled like mad, but achieved nothing, its jaws clamped by the fox's tenacious grip.

In a flash the digger grabbed the fox's brush, twisting and pulling. The fox released its hold, and all three dogs sprang forward. Now I'd heard about Jack Russells, but actually witnessing their killer instinct at work was simply awesome.

The fox was dispatched like lightning. Even the RSPCA would have approved of the speed. And the cubs I'd watched at play were dead almost before they knew what was happening. Within seconds the whole bloody business was over.

This was – and remains – my only experience of Jack Russells hunting foxes. To what extent it was typical I can't naturally say, but the quickness of the kill, reflecting the incredible viciousness of these tiny dogs, left me both grateful and wretched; grateful it was over in no time, wretched the bloodbath had been necessary at all. I suppose it *was* necessary!

And this wasn't the end of the matter, not by a long way. Even the two experienced countrymen were in for a mighty surprise. For Bill put his hand down the crumbling earth, and brought out first one, then another.

Badger cubs.

The two men looked sick with anxiety. They gazed at the cubs, both simply beautiful, and muttered to each other. I couldn't at first hear what they were saying, but Bill soon put me wise. Did I realize it was against the law to harm badgers? In any case this was the last thing Bill at least wanted to do, having sought to protect them all his life. Yet, apart from disturbing their shared tenancy in the fox earth, the cubs were now contaminated by human handling, meaning that the sow would probably kill them.

The two men couldn't understand why there was no sign of her. For a badger with cubs is usually prepared to fight to the death to protect them. Either inexplicably she'd done a bunk or was already dead. Bill notably couldn't have looked more concerned if his own life had been at risk.

'We can't leave 'em here,' he said. So he took them home and – so I gathered – granted his daughter-in-law the inestimable privilege of bottle feeding and handrearing them, at obviously no little inconvenience and cost. I

130

saw them again shortly before they were taken to an animal trust in Norfolk for eventual rehabilitation and release into the wild, both of them brimming with health and absolutely irresistible in their loveliness. How in the world men hunt and bait them with dogs in the name of so-called sport must remain a mystery.

With such goings on, never mind the excitement of the lambing season and its aftermath, serious training for the sheepdog trials, now only a fortnight ahead, had practically ceased. Happy and I had managed to fit in a run or two in the meadow, and I'd made a point of trying to adapt our routine farm activity to sharpen her skills essential for the competition, but otherwise the day to which two months ago I'd constantly looked forward had latterly barely crossed my mind. And when it did, of necessity with growing urgency, my nervousness kept telling me it wasn't worth all the trouble.

What really clinched the matter was when I received a copy of the programme. There at number eight was my name and Happy's, with the other fourteen entrants. The details also indicated that Happy was one of the youngest dogs, much too young, I immediately panicked, for such an ordeal, but remarkably two or three of the others were a good deal younger; and my wife kept reminding me we were entered for novice sheepdog trials, not One Man And His Dog. In any case, Happy's improvement was at times almost sufficient to persuade me she might win!

One day, for example, I decided to separate ewes with twins from those with singles. We'd been very fortunate, averaging virtually one and a half lambs per ewe, and the thought belatedly struck me that the ewes with two mouths to feed were deserving of richer or more plentiful pasture. So Happy and I started to pick off the respective trios, set by set. After the first two or three she saw what was required and completed the job virtually unaided, no fuss, no hurry, simply ignoring the singles as she collected the next trio. What also delighted me was her attitude of firm gentleness, reminiscent of Bill's brother's handling of his dog.

Lapses like nipping and biting, whatever their subtle differences insisted upon by Bill, appeared to belong to the past, barely credible at all.

Most pleasing of all was Happy's new consistency. I've had reason to remark how her performances fluctuated from day to day, sometimes even hour to hour, satisfactory for perhaps a week or more, followed by one disaster after another in erratic sequence. I never did understand it. Bill kept telling me the trouble was *my* inconsistency not the dog's, telling me more often than not, I must add, with sympathy and encouragement. But though accepting he was right, I still suspected that Happy was not entirely without blame. It was one thing for my own frequent exasperations to communicate themselves to the dog, but surely not to the extreme of her ineptitude! When she was good she was very very good, but when she was bad she was diabolical. All this, however, was fading into the past, causing me at times to wonder whether she was ever *that* bad!

As if to confirm my new optimism, three days before the trials Happy completed our miniature course in the meadow without, as far as I could see, a single serious mistake. On the outrun she made a beautiful approach, established firm contact with the sheep for the fetch, and kept them moving steadily straight through the middle of the gates. Ears pricked, tail low, not taking her eyes off her five charges for a moment, she responded like clockwork to each command, at the same time not losing her own initiative to correct trouble almost before it happened.

I felt elated and not a little astonished as she turned the sheep behind me for the drive, pushed on for the second set of gates, then the third, admittedly with the sheep rather less under control, before once more heading for me at the shedding ring. Nothing so far, it seemed to me, was deserving of penalty points, unique in our working relationship.

In the shedding ring the sheep quickly settled, enabling me to manoeuvre a space between two not wearing red collars and the rest, and to call in Happy who moved like lightning. To top it all, she penned them as though any help from me was superfluous, and gave the impression of wanting to start the entire exercise all over again. Sheer magic! True, things didn't go quite so well the very next evening, but I remained sufficiently impressed to be certain that whatever happened at the trials we wouldn't make fools of ourselves.

At first light on the big day Happy as usual was waiting to accompany me to milking. This and other routine jobs out of the way, we returned to the farmhouse for breakfast during which turmoil was even more triumphant than usual. It wasn't merely the children rushing about to feed hens, comb angora rabbits, help to silence the calves bellowing for their breakfast, and mix powdered milk for the lambs, but the whole family's total and noisy abandonment to the excitement of what lay ahead. By the time we reached the trials, a drive of some twelve miles, we were over-ripe for the carnival atmosphere that greeted us.

Happy was on a lead which was just as well for dogs seemed to be everywhere, many of them leadless, and she, I'd just discovered, was coming into season. Otherwise she seemed calm, perhaps a little bewildered by all the activity, but nothing like the agitation that raged beneath my casual exterior.

A tannoy announcement brought me temporary relief from the children's high spirits as they tried to insist I win a sucking pig by throwing a wellington boot the longest distance, utterly undeterred by a youth with the shoulders of an ox who heaved it beyond the carefully arranged measurement area. All competitors for the sheepdog trials were to report as soon as possible at the caravan office!

Standing by the caravan door were seven or eight individuals, each holding a dog, and all but one indecently cheerful in the circumstances. The exception was a young girl, surely not more than fifteen, whose ashen face accentuated her black eyes of misery. I subsequently discovered she was a farmer's daughter taking part in her first trials. Her dog never took his eyes from her, and judging by the way she looked at him there was no doubting their love affair. But, poor girl, she was terrified, reduced to monosyllables and sick laughter.

I should have realized from the programme, but it wasn't until actually standing among these competitors that I appreciated how many women were due to take part. Apart from the teenager they looked of indeterminate age under forty-five. One was a full-time shepherd of limited experience, or so she said, another a farmer's wife, a third an unemployed farm worker, and a fourth my image of a country bumpkin. Her face was like an over-sized rosy apple, bursting with sweetness and appeal, the sort of face that, whatever the weather, bespeaks loaded orchards and sparkling cider. A real country gal, if ever there was one. Later in the day, as we chatted despite her chronic shyness, she told me she was a life-long city girl who worked in a supermarket! More about that in a moment.

As we confirmed our entry the official comforted some of us by explaining we were taking part in the *nursery* novice class, obviously for raw beginners. Again I looked down the programme – Cap (ten months), Nan (fourteen months), Blue (two years), Ladd (nine months), Jake (two years), Fleece (five years), Sam (thirteen months), and so on, Cap the youngest, and a dog named Fly (six years) the eldest. Of the final list of sixteen handlers, six were women.

We all began to chat among ourselves which once more brought me up short as I learned that the over-sized rosy apple's surprising background wasn't at all unique. One man earned his living by managing a saw mill! The others included an accountant, a teacher, a bank clerk, and incredibly to me an airline pilot. But I thought all sheep-dog handlers were professional shepherds! Not on your life, they chorused, this is our *hobby*, the nearest we get to indulging our romanticism about living in the country.

The girl with the rosy-apple face told me she had never lived in the country or wanted to – too quiet and lonely. Her only farming interest was sheepdogs, from the moment some eighteen months ago she'd watched them on TV, and immediately wanted to try. A farmer contacted through a business acquaintance of her father's had sold her a young dog, and also allowed her the use of some of his sheep for training purposes. All the others told similar stories, paying tribute to farmers for lending them sheep while admitting that this aspect of their development as handlers often created problems. The sheep weren't always available when they were, or vice versa, and in some situations an hour with the sheep

135

involved a round journey of three or more hours. Nevertheless the commitment of these city types to their 'shepherding', like their praise of the farmers concerned, was unreserved. 'This is my first trials,' the blooming advertisement for cider informed us; and I was subsequently relieved to learn that the same applied to all but four of the entrants.

In retrospect I'm sorry Happy and I arrived at the course so early. There was so much hanging about! I was occupied enough watching the other competitors, and as I hoped getting the feel of the set-up to steady my nerves, but Happy, despite the children periodically taking her to explore the exhibition of country crafts and numerous sideshows, must have found the long stretches of inactivity something of a trial in themselves.

The sky was overcast after lunch and a wind started to get up, eventually seriously disconcerting the final competitors who shouted or whistled their barely audible commands into the teeth of a gale. But I – and I'm sure Happy – didn't care about the worsening elements; it was such a relief to get started.

The five sheep settled conveniently for Happy to make her outrun from the preferred left, and this she did like a veteran, getting nicely behind them before moving in for a good firm lift. The sheep appeared keen to oblige, gently trotting through the centre of the gates on the fetch, and tightly round the back of me for the drive. There were, inevitably, a number of hiccups, like Happy looking back to me presumably for reassurance, and regaining control of the sheep with too much enthusiasm, but generally her performance so far was, I thought, as good as anything we'd witnessed all day. By comparison with some she was outstanding.

Almost at the first gates on the drive she again stopped

to look back, and three of her charges veered to the left, in fact missed the gates completely as she pushed too hard to correct them. The other two shot through at speed, tried to re-join the trio which further added to the confusion by passing through the gates from the wrong side, taking the two with them, and all five making a beeline for the sideshows at right angles to the second set of gates. For a moment it looked as though things were completely out of hand, but in calm reflection I have to admit that Happy largely corrected the situation on her own.

I shouted against the wind, meaning the dog probably didn't hear me at all, but in any case my growing exasperation and sense of helplessness found expression in little more than heated commands and wild gesticulations.

Eventually Happy collected the five, drove them through the next set of gates, four of them anyway, and kept them moving in a tight bunch to the shedding ring. Ah, yes, the shedding ring! How often had Happy and I separated two of the unmarked sheep in the privacy of the meadow at home. Indeed, how often had we picked off one, two or three sheep from among the entire flock in our routine farming. Yet on this crucial occasion all our carefully rehearsed united efforts were in vain. Belatedly I discovered that for *nursery* novice trials shedding was eliminated as too demanding; each run was concluded with what was thought to be a much simpler requirement – merely penning the sheep!

I set about this task with the innocence befitting my inexperience. Pen five sheep! Nothing to it. Never mind our mini course in the meadow at home, I'd done this sort of thing time without number in day-to-day farming, rarely any trouble, not that you'd notice. I opened the gate, spread myself as far as the rope attached to it would allow, and called in Happy to ease the sheep toward the opening.

She came in all right, with the impatience of a stampeding buffalo. One of the sheep darted round the back, the rest followed like a river bursting its banks, and before I knew what was happening there was pandemonium. The dog hurled after the delinquents, nipped a couple to help them on their indiscriminate way, ignored them to go after the other three which by now were actually off the course altogether, and herself disappeared among the sideshows, whether in search of the sheep or to hide her shame I shall never know.

One thing's for sure – Happy never did link up with the fleeing five again. They had to be rounded up by a retired shepherd and his dog, standing by for such an eventuality, while I listened to a tannoy announcement that the judges had retired me for exceeding the time limit. Yet here's the peculiar thing: some of the comments about Happy by fellow competitors suggested she deserved a prize. And when Bill's brother whose presence I hadn't even known about shook my hand as though we'd just been awarded one my feelings decidedly began to lift.

The real prize winner? The farmer's wife, by a mile. But far more excited or demonstrative was the over-ripe rosy apple, placed third. 'I'm really chuffed,' she told me in surely the understatement of the day. In contrast, the terrified teenager was near to tears. Her dog didn't even reach the sheep on the gather. He kept looking back utterly bewildered. And when, the gale really blowing, she ran toward him to be sure he could hear her commands by whistle he persisted in showing not the slightest interest in the sheep, wanting only to remain with her.

She walked off the course with a brave smile, her dog excitedly jumping around her, illustrating with a vengeance what the official to whom we all reported at the caravan office underlined – that the word novice in novice sheepdog trials refers not to the handler but the dog. I've since learned that this young girl is already quite a shepherd.

Within days the sheepdog trials were forgotten, crashed out of my mind. Happy disappeared. And on the very day she went missing, sheep were savaged on a farm between our village and the next. Naturally it never occurred to me to connect the two disasters – such an idea was unthinkable – but this didn't prevent a call from the police. A dog answering to the description of the one I'd given when reporting Happy missing had been spotted running away from the carnage!

The gentle policeman's response to my indignation – 'I'm only doing my duty, sir' – didn't entirely silence my treacherous doubts centred on the remembrance that Happy's mother had belatedly taken to running off, and according to reports was persisting in her waywardness. Yes, but surely this didn't turn her any more than Happy into a sheep worrier! Such a transformation of character in two otherwise excellent sheepdogs was out of the question.

The next day another savaging took place, this time at a farm nearer our village, with even greater carnage. I'm not sure my informant, our village policeman, wasn't piling on the agony, but his description left nothing to the imagination. 'The sooner this dog is caught and put down,' he said, 'the better.' And I could only agree.

Meanwhile Happy remained missing and increasingly a focal point of suspicion for the police. I kept telling them they were mistaken, but they kept telling me – still in the nicest possible way, mind you – that the rogue dog had the same colouring as my missing dog.

Now as a sheep farmer myself I was hardly likely to view sympathetically any dog, my own included, found guilty of sheep worrying. To witness only one such blood bath, as I had shortly after moving to the country, was enough to understand every farmer's hard-line approach. Most of them wouldn't hesitate to shoot the dog or dogs on sight, no questions asked. Who can blame them! Yet only a short time before Happy's disappearance I'd been compelled to question my own uncompromising attitude, question it, as it were, from the other side of the fence.

Friends of ours on the outskirts of the village finally managed to obtain a magnificent red setter, the sort of dog that even in these parts caused heads to turn. There was no need to remind them about keeping it under strict control in our farming community. Loving everything about country living, not least the lambing season which they were able to watch unfold from the bottom of their spacious garden, they unnecessarily, it was supposed, heightened their fences to be absolutely sure the dog never disturbed the sheep grazing nearby, and twice daily on a lead took it for a romp in the woods. No one could have been more vigilant.

Unfortunately, their excessive caution reckoned without the new arrival's remarkable leaping abilities. One afternoon, their backs turned for a moment, the dog was over the impossible barriers and away, totally indifferent both to their screaming his name and remarkably the sheep in the immediate field.

The husband located the dog within no more than fifteen minutes. It was already in the custody of an angry farmer, a dead lamb at his feet, his flock, many of them yet to lamb, panic stricken and scattered.

Abject apologies and an immediate offer of financial compensation did nothing to abate the farmer's fury; the police were informed and a summons issued. If these friends of ours had been strangers I too, make no mistake, assuming the dog was out of control because of their negligence, wouldn't have hesitated to seek retribution to the limit.

The reality from *their* standpoint was somewhat different. They sent the farmer his compensatory demand, no argument about the figure, turned their garden into a veritable Fort Knox, worried themselves sick about their appearance in court and its possible outcome for the dog, and felt as guilty as hell. In the event they were fined £50 with costs, given a dire warning, and lectured like criminals.

I've no wish to minimize their guilt; they did after all fail to keep their dog under control. And my sympathies remain with the farmer. But the situation from the inside, as I knew it, looked rather different from the evidence, the objective facts, presented in court.

Now here I was with the same haunting accusations being aimed at my dog and of course at me! The only difference so far between their case and mine was that their dog undoubtedly tossed a lamb and broke its neck, whereas mine was no more than missing and under suspicion.

The uncertainty continued for another three days. Then I received a phone call from the police – Happy was in their custody, brought in by a man who'd found her in his garden. Why hadn't he seen my name and phone number on her collar? The dog hadn't been wearing a collar! But she was never without it, I insisted.

Not wasting a moment I jumped into the car and made for the police station. Happy was crouched on the floor, her eyes dripping with anxiety. Even when I called she hesitated, unsure, almost cowed, an attitude I'd never seen in her before. The policeman noticed, and pointedly made a reference. Had she ever been beaten? he asked, rubbing behind her ears. She rolled on her back, like a gesture of submission, her eyes reflecting her total attitude of fear, foreboding. Like a whipped dog!

Checking the paper work, the policeman excused himself to answer the phone through a hatch connecting the main office. Happy again rolled on her back as I knelt to stroke her head and stomach. She shuffled closer, dragging her collapsed hind quarters with her front paws. Wretchedness was written all over her. I gathered her in my arms and tried to communicate the joy I felt at her return.

The policeman put down the phone, and turned smiling. 'That should get you off the hook,' he said, and explained that the call had been about another savaging within the past half hour. Nevertheless I was required to answer more questions, provide yet more information, give more and more details, as though my interrogator was trying to prove that what he had just told me didn't apply. Another dog of Happy's colouring sighted at the scene of the crime or not, he appeared to be going out of his way to emphasize he for one wasn't convinced of Happy's innocence. In retrospect I realize he was simply doing his job, doing it with commendable thoroughness, but at the time his persistent questioning seemed both unnecessary and finally offensive.

On the way home, Happy still inconsolably subdued, my relief was mingled with puzzlement and concern little short of panic. What had made her run off? It didn't make sense, at least not to me. And if she'd gone once she might go again. And again. Why, why, why? throbbed in my mind.

Incredibly the obvious explanation never remotely occurred to me, until my wife brought to my notice a slight discolouring on the kitchen floor. Of course! Happy had disappeared in search of a mate. How else did I imagine she'd respond to this most fundamental of urges? And I'd known she was coming into season! My stupidity was unforgivable.

The implications of her running off, on the other hand, barely took a moment to register. In the first place I didn't want her to whelp so young, perhaps the next time round but certainly not this time; and secondly, assuming my worst fears were confirmed, which of the many dogs in the neighbourhood was the father? Not a sheepdog, I was pretty sure, otherwise one of my neighbours would have let me know Happy was hanging about his farm.

I phoned the man who'd found her. Did he have a dog? A black labrador. Did he know whether the dogs had mated? Inexplicably he roared with laughter. 'My dog,' he finally controlled himself, 'disappeared too for a couple of days, so putting one and one together,' his amusement again exploded, 'I wouldn't be a bit surprised.' Not entirely appreciating his sense of humour I phoned the vet for an appointment.

The beloved man, noted for calling a spade a spade, was decidedly not amused either. Surely I knew my own dog was in season? I did. Then why hadn't I been more careful? I mumbled something about it never having occurred to me Happy might run off. He shrugged his shoulders, and rose dismissively; as far as he was concerned the consultation was over. But I don't want her to whelp, I explained, she's too young. And anyway the puppies of the dog with whom she'd almost certainly mated would be too big for uncomplicated delivery. In these special circumstances couldn't something be done, in fairness to Happy?

His eyes filled with disapproval bordering on contempt. I don't normally do this sort of thing, he snapped, if I do it this time don't come back if she runs off again. And not trying to hide his opinion of irresponsible dog owners, he picked up a syringe, explaining the injection would nullify any existing conception and recommence Happy's oestrous cycle. This means, a belligerent smile surfaced, you'll need to watch her for three weeks, just to be sure! The frightened schoolboy within me stammered thanks and bolted with Happy to the exit.

Outside I bumped into my other interrogator, the arm of the law, visiting the vet, he said, on official business. He rubbed Happy behind the ears, told me she was a super dog, and laughingly assured me he'd never for a moment really suspected she was the sheep worrier in the first place. He certainly fooled me! I left his presence like a reprieved man walking to freedom.

As things turned out I didn't have time to brood. The very next morning I woke early, or more likely was awakened, to hear peculiar noises coming from what sounded like the other side of the barn. Half asleep I peered through the bedroom window, and seriously wondered whether I was dreaming. Four of our bigger calves were loose, galloping, cavorting, kicking their hind legs high in the air, tearing about like children let out to play after being restrained for too long.

My wife crept to my side, confirmed I wasn't dreaming, yawned, muttered something about our own rodeo show, and climbed back into bed. I grabbed my wellies at the kitchen door and rushed out to investigate.

Mystery. The calves were definitely in the field, but there was no sign of a breakout from the barn. Every pen was secure, seemingly invulnerable. The younger calves still on milk, assuming I'd arrived with an early breakfast, bellowed a welcome. Otherwise I was left in peace to cogitate about the escape.

For your understanding I have to direct attention to the mountain of wholesome dung and straw festering near the cowshed, landmark of my prowess at mucking out, the inescapable chore, you remember, I love to hate. Healthy animals always leave evidence of their remarkable eating capacity, and such evidence requires removal from sty, stall, and barn.

As far as the calves were concerned I'd fairly recently adopted a new system. Pressurized by the lambing season, and with the milder weather making the release of the calves to free pasture only a matter of weeks away, I stopped removing the old bedding weekly, and simply spread the new on top. Once the barn was free I planned to use the tractor with digger attachment to shift the lot in one go.

What I overlooked was that if I was too generous with the fresh bedding I was effectively reducing the height of the pens in the barn. Doubtless the calves couldn't believe their luck. Fed up with being inside throughout the winter, they used the elevated floor to leap to freedom. Their crazy rushing about was nothing more than their pent-up exuberance exercising itself. Lovely to behold, and made me sad to have to return them inside for a little longer, but at least they enjoyed the morning as I restored the floor to its normal proportions.

When after all these exertions I returned to our now hopefully dog-proof garden, Happy was investigating a hedgehog, rolled up tight at her nose. The only thing I knew about hedgehogs concerned their massive reputation for fleas. Lousy from this standpoint they might be, but otherwise they're fascinating creatures, as I soon discovered.

I came across one, probably the same one, shuffling around on the boundary of the garden. Whatever could Thomas Hardy have meant when he wrote:

> Some nocturnal blackness, mothy and warm,
> When the hedgehog travels furtively over the lawn.

Furtively? This one positively swaggered as though he owned the place. Grunting and sniffing, he searched for food, spasmodically stopping to relish worm or slug. I thoughtlessly watched too close. He curled up, hiding his face and soft underbelly, erecting his prickly defence, guarantee of safety in our setting but ironically fatal elsewhere. For caught in the beams of a car he rolls up on the spot, an unmissable victim. On this occasion, however, he soon uncurled, and went on snuffling and snorting, seemingly famished after his long hibernation.

I'm told hedgehogs love snails more than anything. If they find one their sharp teeth, as I witnessed, crack the shell in no time and dispatch the morsel with noisy pleasure. Rather like a bad mannered gourmand.

Whether this same one was involved a few nights later I'm not to know, but a pair of them, bearing in mind Philip Toynbee's remark that making love is two bodies laughing together, were roaring their heads off. Yes, I've heard the old chestnut about how do hedgehogs make love? Carefully. But this doesn't alter the fact that they get on with it with gusto.

At the time I didn't realize that hedgehogs are utterly promiscuous. Fortuitous encounter is the only requirement of ready coupling. Almost inevitably this isn't all.

The males have absolutely nothing to do with either the actual birth of their offspring or their rearing. Everything is left to the females. Strange how the principle of evolutionary enlightenment doesn't seem to apply in this area. The females presumably don't object. The males enthusiastically oblige, and move on to further mating delights uncomplicated by family responsibilities.

Why is it that some animals are monogamous, faithful for life, shattered like the swan when the partner dies, while others like the hedgehog . . . ? Such questions never cease to intrigue me, though I'm no nearer any answers, specially since learning that even swans are now suspected of occasional wife swopping!

Another conundrum of a different kind confronted me a few weeks later, shortly after dawn. The day before, peace and harmony ruled. Sheep basked in the sun, only bestirring themselves to let their lambs suckle. The lambs themselves raced and frolicked, totally unsuspecting. The calves, thriving on lush summer pasture, peered content-edly over a fence, doubtless puzzled as to why the entire family advancing up the adjacent field appeared at such cross purposes.

Having sent Happy to bring on the whole flock, I asked my wife and children to spread themselves on the open approach to a pen alongside the cowshed. Within minutes the penning was complete. So far so good. All that remained was to put the lot through a single-file exit leading to a separating gate where I picked off the lambs and let the sheep through. It went like clockwork, apart, that is, from the bedlam.

The ewes baaed for their lambs. The lambs baaed for their mums. One of the children was knocked flying as the leader of the flock tried to jump the pen to her lamb.

Imagine scores of alley cats on the rampage, and you have the picture. To make matters worse, the children, desperately sorry for the lambs, frowned in my direction.

Farmer friends assured us that the racket of weaning wouldn't last long, and naturally they were right. It just seemed longer, unending, in fact. Still, with the sheep on the far side of the farm, and the lambs separated from them by two large fields, we tried to be philosophical; tried with little initial success. The lambs were too near the farmhouse to make their protests less than ear splitting. And the gentle darkness did nothing to soothe them.

Much later than usual my wife and I wearily climbed into bed, but sleep was impossible. Tossing and turning we couldn't escape the hullabaloo, and wished by some magic the sheep and lambs could be made to realize the futility of their lament.

All too soon it was time to get up. Eyes fighting to stay open, I strained to listen. Not a solitary baa to challenge the dawn chorus! Heavenly. I whispered to my wife that the sheep and lambs had already accepted their separation. Her only response was to threaten me with one if I didn't let her get some sleep.

The kettle was soon singing on the boil for coffee. Sipping to induce life, I oozed goodwill to man and beast. Rarely had silence sounded so benevolent. Counting my blessings I stepped resolutely out of the farmhouse to do the milking, Happy responding to my enthusiasm at such a glorious day. The sun was up, birds were singing. Marvellous to be alive!

Casually my bleary eyes checked the lambs. I blinked hard, and steadied myself to take a long hard look. Suddenly the sky darkened, the tail end of the dawn chorus mocked. Lambs were suckling, dancing, playfully butting; sheep were grazing contentedly, their crafty leader pausing to glance in my direction, I swear, to laugh. Reunion celebrations were well and truly underway. All that remained was to repair the holes in the fences, and repeat the whole miserable business. In the event we decided to wait a day or two, to catch up on our sleep.

Even when the separation was again completed, this time on a permanent basis, our tribulations with the lambs proved to be anything but over. A day or two after they'd stopped complaining about being separated from their mums, Happy and I were doing one of our daily routine checks. A lamb in the distance caught my eye. I stared hard, and my heart sank.

Ironically, until that moment I could hardly have felt more carefree; utterly in love with life, confident the whole universe was governed by a fundamental benevolence. The early sun promised another glorious summer's day, while a gentle breeze, warm yet refreshing, was rapidly drying the surprisingly heavy dew. It was, in other words, the sort of day that turns the entire countryside into a Constable painting, and makes the chance to work on the land a privilege surely beyond price.

My eyes, as I say, casually roamed the bounty of the lambing season, picking out triplets and twins, all of them strong and lusty, some after a less than promising start. Naturally this added to my sense of pleasure bordering on smug self-satisfaction.

More encouraging still were certain singles, not the ones well above average from the moment they were born, but the half dozen or so most weakly whose survival at all was something of a bonus. Watching their merry-making, I was almost purring.

Then I spotted this lamb! It was more agitated than frisky, a subtle distinction I find hard to put into words

149

without obscuring its reality and significance. Happy followed to heel as I advanced, not for a moment taking my eyes off the lamb, increasingly fearful something was wrong or at best far from right.

Away to me, I whispered; and Happy shot off to make a perfect pear-shaped approach, bringing on all the lambs and holding them in a corner of the field hard by the gate and a hedge.

It wasn't too difficult – the second time, I admit – to collar the lamb I wanted with my shepherd's crook, incidentally a Christmas gift from my wife, beautifully carved by an old shepherd in Wales, and perfectly proportioned for grabbing either a lamb's neck or a sheep's hock.

I picked up the lamb, by now big enough to struggle awkwardly, examined its back end, and swallowed hard. Forget the lovely day and the supposedly fundamental benevolence, I felt sick. The lamb's rump was a heaving mass of maggots.

'Fly!' I groaned out loud. And that one word underlined how a simple development on a family farm like ours can shatter in a moment not only one's sense of infinite well-being but also double the work load for days and possibly weeks to come.

Before coming here I'd heard of fly fishing, and appreciated the skill involved on the couple of occasions I'd watched an expert casting. I'd also heard of a fly farm where thousands of gallons of maggots are produced weekly for angling enthusiasts. But a lamb with fly! This was something else, believe me.

Scouring or diarrhoea gives this dreaded disease its opportunity by providing an ideal breeding ground for the blowfly among soiled wool near the anus. And each adult fly, though its life-span is little more than a month, is capable of laying sizeable batches of eggs on a number of lambs and sheep.

The larvae hatch rapidly, and feed on live flesh, eating their way further and further into the helpless victim. Then they drop off, form a pupa in the soil, and emerge after a few weeks as adult flies to start the whole gruesome cycle all over again.

Mature sheep are not so easily infected, first because their immunity is naturally stronger, and second regular dagging (arse trimming) reduces the chance of their wool getting soiled even if diarrhoea, less likely in any case with age, proves to be a problem.

Incredibly, despite my watching the flock like a hawk especially with fly in mind, the hole in the lamb's raw rump was already the size of my fist. No wonder the poor little blighter was more agitated than frisky, for fly is notorious for the speed with which it brings its victims down, turning within hours a joyful tearaway lamb into a pathetic shadow of its former self. And unless treated quickly, death is inevitable.

Pulling out my knife, I flicked off all the easily removable maggots, and carried the lamb to the farm workshop cum surgery for emergencies of this nature. Decidedly not hurrying but not wasting a moment, I removed the congealed shit and dirt, scraped out the maggots, and dabbed the whole tender area with disinfectant. Then I plunged the lamb into a tank of sheep dip, holding it there for a thorough soaking.

Nagging at the back of my mind all the time was the cause of the scouring or diarrhoea in the first place. Either the lamb had eaten too much grass or – more likely – was suffering from roundworm, another hazard theoretically countered by regular injections six weeks after birth and every six weeks until the autumn. Yes, but I'd done this conscientiously for the entire flock, and also, I believed, changed their grazing often enough to reduce if not eliminate the risk of roundworm infection.

You see, the eggs of roundworm are laid inside the stomach or bowels of the sheep, and pass out with their droppings. Within twenty-four hours these become larvae which some three to seven days later are sufficiently developed to infect other grazing sheep. The only way to prevent a build-up of larvae is to rotate frequently, before the microbe is ready to perpetuate its dirty work, plus, of course, the stipulated dosing. Well, I'd paid attention to both, so where had I gone wrong?

Was it possible, I asked myself, that this lamb with fly had somehow been overlooked at the last injections? To be honest, I hoped so, otherwise, if the pasture itself was heavily infected with larvae, all the lambs, not to mention the sheep, were highly vulnerable. No wonder my heart sank.

I immediately brought the dosing forward by two weeks and determined to change the pasture every other day, realizing, at the same time, that even this wouldn't resolve the problem if the fields were already heavily contaminated.

Within a couple of days another lamb went down with fly, then another, and a third; but remarkably no more. Nevertheless, why is it the dreaded blowfly persists in proving stronger than all the precautions? Dose and dip as often as recommended by the experts, it still happens that lambs and occasionally sheep are brought low by this ghastly infection.

Unfortunately, lambs being eaten alive weren't our only trouble at this suddenly hectic period. And to avoid possible misunderstanding as I try to explain, let me at the outset make clear that normally, all things considered, I love pigs. Like Happy herself, they are clever, clean – yes, fastidiously clean about their bedding area – and touchingly responsive to affection. Nothing pleases them more than having their backs scratched. Sheer bliss. No question, the perfect embodiment of happiness is a pig having its back scratched.

But never at feed time! Hearing the buckets approaching they go berserk – squeal like crazy and lunge the full weight of their impatience against the door, just to assure the bearer of a welcome.

Well, the morning I discovered the third lamb suffering from fly, thoroughly discouraged, wondering how many more, I warily unbolted the first door of our twin sties, and stepped aside sharpish. As usual the sow charged out, and almost immediately turned on herself to chase me (or rather the bucket) in. This crucial respite, barely more than a couple of seconds, enabled me to pour enough nourishment into the trough to keep her occupied while I completed the pouring at the other end, relatively unmolested.

The cat-on-hot-bricks operation was repeated in the adjacent sty, no problem. Casually I turned to go. Confronting me in the doorway and still resolutely advancing was the nemesis of my having overlooked to slip the bolt next door. The intruder, having scoffed her own ample rations, was looking for more, and clearly in no mood to take no for an answer.

Now there's one thing a pig can't stand, I've discovered: the smell of another pig. Once their smells mingle, get really acquainted, they're the best of friends, but until then mutual spiteful detestation rules. Number one pig barged her way to the trough of number two pig, an

153

affront in itself, at which point their smells collided. All hell was let loose!

Squeals, grunts, noises of the underworld, fire and brimstone, the lot. Round and round the sty they went, with me desperately trying to get out of the way and at the same time separate the inseparable.

No wonder pigs are sometimes called swine.

If I mention that I finally managed to get the intruder out by kicking her up the backside you must believe it was for her own good and my respect for life. Principally my own. Not that this helped overmuch. Ignoring her own door she advanced to an outer one leading straight into the farmyard, totally indifferent to Happy who was snoozing directly in the way.

The dog, alerted by my shouts, and persuaded by my hot pursuit that the sow was heading for prohibited territory, foolishly made no attempt to remove herself. On the contrary, faithful to the last, she resolutely blocked the troublemaker's only means of escape. I could do nothing to warn her.

She hit the mud with a howl of protest, picked herself up, and – not hesitating for a moment – hurled herself at the sow. The next half minute made the bloody encounter of five minutes before a lovers' tiff by comparison. I can only surmise that when Happy went into action she didn't doubt that the sow, like lamb, sheep, housecow or even bull, would back off or at least show *some sign* of intimidation. Her disillusionment came too late!

The sow aimed her massive weight at the dog, and once having launched herself was in no position anyway to turn aside. Happy again picked herself up, clearly couldn't believe such ignominy, and bravely decided discretion was the better part of valour. She moved behind me, and glared defiance from the barricade of my backside.

This capitulation was seemingly enough to satisfy honour on both sides, for the grunting sow made no further attempt to reach the dog, while Happy herself continued courageously to peer through my legs. I'd never doubted her intelligence, and here was proof positive!

Having calmed down, the undisputed champ of the farmyard was soon amiable enough gently to be directed back to her sty, directed, incidentally, by nothing more than a small square of plywood used both to restrict her vision and focus the way I wanted her to take. Sounds simple, but in my experience it never fails.

Pigs certainly have a mind of their own, and can be really nasty, but normally they are the friendliest and most co-operative of animals, evidence, I'm sure, of their remarkable intelligence. I reckon the average sow would make a first-class sheepdog. They're fearless enough (ask Happy!) with beast or man (as I can testify), notably when it comes to fulfilling their own gluttonous ends; but they might experience difficulty in sustaining adequate herding speed if the sheep were awkward, and undoubtedly their lack of strong gentleness when roused could create a problem or two. On balance, I think I'll stick with Happy, in the same way, I imagine, as Happy will stick with sheep or housecows or bullocks or even bulls; never, however, pigs. What an exceptionally clever girl!

I did, though, seriously doubt her intelligence, never mind my own, on what proved shortly afterwards to be the worst farming day of our lives, the stuff of which inescapable nightmares are made. And ironically the day couldn't have started more promisingly. But let me go back to the very beginning.

Before we arrived here, starry-eyed and largely clueless, we romanticized about nothing more than the haymaking. You can imagine! Sunny days of cutting and fluffing the hay, baling it into neat parcels of sweet-smelling winter nourishment for the stock, gathering the bales on a tractor-drawn trailer, the pile rising higher and higher, wife and children bubbling with fun on the top. Sheer bliss! And *then* the prospect of actually building our own haystack virtually in our own backyard!

The only reason we hesitated to start was remembrance of what happened shortly after we moved in. Our neighbour, member of a farming family for generations, noted for his local weather forecasts, drove his cutter into one of his fields the size of two of ours, and began. A couple of brief runs as he adjusted something on the machine, and he was away, round and round, an artist at work, a joy to watch.

The sun was too fierce for comfort in the tractor cabin as he began the fourth or fifth round, but even before he completed it clouds angrily gathered, lightning flashed, and the heavens opened. Out of the blue, as it were, a storm of tropical proportions.

My assumption was that he would immediately stop; surely no point in carrying on. But – thunder roaring, rain like stair rods exposing the inadequacy of his windscreen wiper – he continued his merry way as though the sun was still shining, leaving in his wake hay thoroughly sodden even before it was cut, and now almost awash.

Shortly before he finished, the sun once more began to smile, and soon the glorious day that prompted him to make a start was restored. A sad irony. Yet undeterred he smiled and waved as he rattled his way back to his farmyard, apparently unconcerned about the unexpected outcome of his morning's work.

And next morning, still smiling and waving, he was back this time with a machine to fluff up the hay. By mid-afternoon it was gently steaming in the powerful sun. He repeated the whole exercise twice more, but it was still more than a week before the hay was sufficiently dried out for baling and stacking.

So understandably we were wary about starting our own haymaking the following year. Scanning the sky and compulsively listening to every weather forecast on the radio, it was nevertheless difficult to decide, difficult, that is, until we saw our neighbour's cutter once more rumbling to his field next to ours. Never mind his miscalculation of last year, this was clearly no time for the faint hearted.

Routine chores hurriedly out of the way, I hitched our ancient cutter to the tractor, and headed from the farmyard. As usual Happy was crouched in the cab in a place seemingly made for her comfort and convenience. My wife, a bucket in each hand as she struggled toward the more draught proof of our two smaller barns to feed our youngest calves, shouted be careful, commonsense in the circumstances seeing this was to be my first experience of cutting hay.

I reached the gate, nipped out to open it, and noticed that Happy, not so much as by your leave, was haring toward two of the children playing in a nearby spinney. Vaguely I saw them fussing her, but was too preoccupied about the mowing to give it a second thought. By the way, I realize I'm being rather ponderous with such details, but they're essential for your understanding of the disaster ahead.

My initial two or three times round the field were exhilarating. Admittedly progress was exceedingly slow, but my sense of achievement had me singing at the top of my voice. This was the life! The tractor purred, the hay fell like ninepins, on the whole without too much zigzagging. As the morning wore on, however, pleasure gave way to disenchantment. Forget the sweltering heat in the cabin, the fumes from the engine alone guaranteed a progressively uncomfortable ride, and when to this was added a splitting headache caused by my inexperience demanding unrelieved concentration I began to have second thoughts about the reputed fun of haymaking.

Each time I passed the children, swinging from trees in the spinney, my cheery response to their waves belied my feelings. Lunch seemed ages ahead. I began to feel sick. My head thumped. And each time round the field only emphasized how many more circuits were needed.

What happened next – out of nowhere – I shall never fully understand or forget. Happy let out a terrible yelp. I looked down, jammed on the brakes, and shot off my seat.

She was in a pool of blood, one leg almost severed, the pad of another hanging by the skin, the other two badly mangled and cut. I picked her up, ran to the van in the farmyard, and drove like mad to the vet's.

That journey is seared in my memory. Blood was everywhere. I didn't know whether to try to staunch the flow or put my foot down. Happy herself lay in her customary place in front of the passenger seat, her soft eyes full of bewilderment – FEAR. Occasionally she whimpered, but otherwise remained quiet and still. Indeed, she couldn't move, in any case made no attempt; just lay staring at me doubtless wondering why I was doing nothing to help.

Long before we reached the vet's six miles away she was trembling all over and looking more dead than alive. Temporary traffic lights at road repairs kept us waiting –

no more than half a minute but it seemed like hours. I pleaded with those lights to change, PLEADED; and drove the final couple of miles much faster than I should, like a madman, in fact, urged on by the terrible dread Happy was going to die.

Clients with their pets quietly waited their turn, but seeing my clothes soaked with blood must have understood as I strode straight into the consulting room. The vet examined Happy, applied a tourniquet to the nearly severed leg, and told me he'd deal with the other clients as quickly as possible.

Impatiently I waited – wretched, despairing; as guilty as hell. Happy, the farm's pride and joy, loyal, affectionate, utterly dependable – and now this. I tried to fathom what in the world could have happened. One moment, as far as I knew, Happy was playing with the children, the next entangled with the cutter. It didn't make sense. She wasn't stupid, the very opposite, yet somehow she'd wandered unnoticed into the danger area. And why hadn't I seen her? My headache was no excuse. There *was* no excuse.

Yes, yes, but where precisely had she come from? The way from the spinney was already cut, offering me a clear view. And why, whatever the direction of her approach, had she plunged into the cutter? The more I thought about it, the less sense it all made.

Happy meanwhile never took her eyes off me. No whimpering now – just a look of pain; and accusation? I was choked. In the grip of desolating helplessness.

At last I carried her into the surgery, and for what seemed like hours the vet worked – stitching, more stitching, and still more; reassuring the dog, telling me the outcome was bound to be uncertain. She might never walk again, certainly without a heavy limp. As for working the sheep, it would be wise to act on the assumption . . .

But he kept stitching, his gentle hands firmly sorting out the bloody mess. First the near severed leg, then the near severed pad, then the other two, neither anything like as bad but still cut to ribbons.

Eventually it was done. The dog remained perfectly still, as uncomplaining as she had been co-operative throughout the long operation. Her eyes never left me. Mine, I confess, were full of tears – and remorse and hopelessness.

'Keep her sedated,' the good man said as he finished the bandaging.

I muttered thanks, and he must have read my thoughts. 'This kind of thing happens often,' he tried to console me, 'don't blame yourself. Only the other day I had a pig with its legs sheared clean off; farmer cutting his orchard. These things are bound to happen.'

Not my fault! I wanted to believe him, did, in fact, believe him with my head. But my feelings told me otherwise, screamed accusations for which there were no excuses. I was guilty. A bit less self-pity on that bloody tractor, splitting headache or not, and this might never have happened.

Tenderly I carried Happy to the van, placed her in the passenger seat, and drove home trying to avoid every suggestion of a bump in the road. The unmade-up farm track from what we extravagantly call our main road to the farmyard, getting on for three quarters of a mile, was agony for me, let alone Happy. Not that she complained. The only indication of pain was the haunted look in her eyes which continued to focus appealingly on me.

As we crawled into the farmyard the entire family came running, and one glimpse was enough to confirm

160

their worst fears. Despite the sedation Happy was still alert as I eased her into her box by the kitchen stove. Two of her bandages were already soaked, one of them dripping, yet Happy herself gave the impression – and I'm honestly trying to avoid sentimentality – that her own condition was the least of her concerns. She seemed almost cowed, as though apologetic for causing so much trouble. Nuzzling into my face, she licked me, gently wagged her tail as if not sure of my approval, and even attempted to shuffle forward, trying to demonstrate she wasn't completely helpless. Needless to say, her courage and general attitude added to my wretchedness.

What also surprised me was the reaction of the children, notably one of the two playing in the spinney. While her sisters wept copiously, her tearless eyes shone with desperation. Just before going to bed she helped to change Happy's bandages, and, saying nothing to anyone, got up in the night to check the dog was as comfortable as could be expected. Furthermore she was the lone voice which quietly insisted from the onset that Happy would walk and run again. I hadn't the heart to disillusion her.

But after a few days I began to wonder whether I and the other jeremiahs in the family were the ones requiring to be disillusioned. For Bill Wheel called, took one look at the dog, and pontificated (no other word will do) that she would get over it in no time. Normally Bill no more exaggerates than displays uninhibited optimism, but on this occasion his confidence was absolute. At least. To say I was heartened is an understatement, particularly as he asserted his opinion as little short of a threat to anyone inclined to disagree.

Even so, I couldn't get the vet's forebodings out of my mind. And when, as the weeks slipped by, Happy herself offered little encouragement that Bill's prophecy was likely to come true, I began to suspect that the old countryman's heart had ruled his usually wise head. The only times she left her box was to be carried outside for obvious reasons; and finding it impossible to stand once on the grass, her predicament can be imagined.

But I'm racing ahead of my story. Before any of this began to unfold, the mowing awaited completion. The day of the accident I hadn't the heart to return to it, and the next day was no easier. Fortunately the weather held, unlike my resolve to get back to the mowing and finish it quickly.

I woke after another restless night, groped my way into the kitchen, and was confronted by an implication of the accident I never anticipated would hurt so much. Instead of the customary excited greeting Happy gave me each morning, she barely stirred in her box; just gazed longingly as I made my way to the door. And the walk to the cowshed, usually involving just the pair of us, was the loneliest of my life. Funny thing, until then I didn't really know what it was to be lonely, even when on my own for long stretches. But that short walk from the farmhouse to the cowshed somehow brought home to me how different life was going to be without Happy's constant companionship. I didn't merely feel lopsided and incomplete but a cripple within myself, as though I'd had the accident. Rather like, I suppose, someone grieving the severance of a limb. I knew I loved my dog, but this depth of desolation, I must confess, took me completely by surprise.

During the milking, and later feeding the pigs, hens and ducks, I found myself looking for Happy all the time, occasionally, momentarily forgetful, calling to her. Worse still, of course, was when I went to check the sheep and lambs. Without Happy in attendance I was cackhanded, reduced to near impotence or compelled to do ten times the work simply to examine any suspected victim of fly.

A lamb's apathetic behaviour, for instance, indicated a closer look was essential. I made a couple of lunges with my crook but – despite the docility – the lamb was too nippy for me. So we were back to the need of human sheepdogs. Out of the farmhouse tumbled the less than enthusiastic family whose ineptitude hadn't improved without practice. Chaos ruled – OK.

Eventually I managed to pick off the cause of all this shouting and mutual recrimination, only to discover that fly certainly was not the reason behind the lamb's uncharacteristic behaviour. Actually, I never did trace the trouble, and in the light of how the lamb subsequently developed now doubt that it ever existed at all, apart from in my imagination. But you see how Happy's absence paradoxically made it impossible for me to get away from her.

This experience with the lamb was itself sufficient for me to look at Patch's training programme, but first, of even more immediate concern, was the need to finish the mowing, now irrationally hanging over me like a guarantee of further disaster. And in fact these fears were fulfilled almost immediately I re-started.

The cutter was put out of action by a stone jamming between two blades and shearing them off. Getting replacements for an ancient model like ours proved to be a problem! Meanwhile our neighbour's posh mower sped round all his fields in what seemed like less than no time, leaving me still stuck in our first.

However, by late supper on the following day I too had finished, and that night, the children safely tucked in bed, my wife and I strolled among the new mowed hay, picking up handfuls, burying our noses in it, telling each other its smell was as fresh as bread straight from the oven. Marvellous.

The next stage in haymaking was to fluff up the hay to be sure it was absolutely dry before baling and stacking. Some farmers don't bother with this, convinced if they cut in the right weather conditions it isn't necessary, but the example of our neighbour, quite apart from Bill Wheel's advice, left us in no doubt.

As with mowing, turning looks simple or straightforward enough, but is really an acquired art. No use merely fluffing up the hay. It also needs to be in a straight line, to facilitate the baling; and with a baler as antagonistic as ours we can't afford the slightest deviation.

Well, I finished the turning in a day, no real problems, and, reassured by the weather forecast, decided to leave it for two or three days before baling. At least as much on my mind was the next visit to the vet's with Happy. In the intervening days since the accident she had shown a growing disinclination to take notice of anyone or anything going on around her, finally barely stirring at all at the approach of either myself or her chief nurse among the children.

The only times she sparked up was first thing each morning as I emerged from the bedroom, as though my appearance at first light put before her the prospect of our working together like old times. But reality quickly intervened as first her enthusiasm was curbed by her useless feet, and then snuffed out completely as I left the farmhouse alone.

The vet was no more hopeful. Or – to be fair – hope empty. It was, he said, too early to say, either way. The cuts were healing, but he couldn't be sure about the mangled tendons and muscles. Time alone would tell. In the meanwhile I was to keep her mildly sedated, and in no circumstances encourage her to stand. She would know when she was ready. Patience was the key word. After all, we were fortunate the dog had survived!

We told the children the vet's report wasn't too bad. Whereupon Happy's chief nurse among them rounded on all of us for our lack of faith, insisting she knew more about it than the vet. Shortly afterwards my wife found her in the dairy weeping tears of barely acknowledged doubt.

In retrospect I'm glad we had the haymaking to worry about. Almost gratefully we turned to the baler, a museum piece bought from a neighbour for a song, and reputedly still in working order. Theoretically it scooped up the hay, crushed it into neat oblong parcels tied longways on both sides by an automatic stringer, and dropped them off the back at regular intervals for carting.

We began – my wife driving the tractor, I keeping my eye on the baler – immediately she returned from taking the children to school. Within minutes I was swallowing dust, spitting stubble, and battling with too many untied pieces of twine. But who cared? The field was slowly filling with the crucial difference between sparse winter rations for the animals and PLENTY.

We pushed on with only two brief stops, one for lunch, the other while the children were collected from school. Otherwise round and round at a snail's pace, the baler clanging its protest as it defied every law of logic to keep going. Three weary days later we were ready for the great gathering in, a festive occasion, as we planned it!

A number of our new friends in the village offered to help – indeed, pleaded for the privilege – and a family of old friends, still confirmed townees but anxious to find out what we were up to, turned down flat our offer to postpone their week-end visit when we mentioned it clashed with the haymaking. On the contrary, their innocent enthusiasm knew no bounds.

We all lugged the bales to collecting points for stacking on the trailer and transportation to the barn, the women quickly proving their equality not only at carrying the bales but throwing them to my wife whose dexterity at stacking, learned by nothing more than trial and error, surprised the retired farm worker who helped as general supervisor.

Everybody worked with at least as much laughter as application, my wife meanwhile going higher and higher, finally too high for comfort. Yet as soon as she gave the signal the children clambered to join her for the precarious journey to the barn. They squealed with delight as the mobile haystack swayed, and just as noisily simulated fear as their heads missed decapitation by inches as they passed under a main beam into the Tyler barn.

By lunch time most of us were sore not only from sunburn and the twine of the bales cutting into our hands, but from muscles not previously suspected. What some of us would have done without the reviving properties of home made bread and our own farm butter and cheese I don't know. In any case, within the hour we were all uncomplainingly back on the treadmill, clearing load after load, until – completely knackered – we heaved the final bales into place on the haystack, shortly before sunset. By then the only ones disappointed among us were the children who wanted haymaking to go on forever.

Looking back, the whole day for me at least was therapeutic. For not only did it take my mind off the dog, it also lifted my spirits to such an extent I never did wholly return to my former gloom. Not that I wasn't still sick at heart, haunted by a wretchedness that followed me everywhere, my guilt renewed each time I entered the farmhouse kitchen to be confronted by a pair of eyes full of hurt and longing. The thought wouldn't go away – whatever had I been doing to allow such a calamity?

The answer only slowly began to fall into place. As far as I could make out, Happy had become thoroughly excitable playing with the children in the spinney, tearing after them as they'd swung on a rope from a magnificent oak, incidentally one of their favourite games. My waving to them each time I passed with the mower had apparently caused Happy a degree of indecision. Should she follow me or continue to enjoy the antics of the children? Once or twice, they said, she'd set off but soon turned back; and when eventually she did hare off they hadn't given it a second thought.

Yes, but why, even in this playful mood, had she plunged straight into the cutters? It was only then I realized that when working almost flat on the ground they were virtually hidden by the hay.

The vet continued to exonerate me, though this didn't help. I knew I should have taken greater care. Yet even with hindsight I wasn't clear precisely how. To lock or chain up Happy would never have occurred to me; and I was already mindful of the lethal nature of the mower. I'd drummed into the children the need to keep well clear, warning them not even to come into the field I was cutting.

Then why hadn't it crossed my mind that Happy might also be at risk? Such cogitations didn't really help, and at the end of the day I was always left with the same question – why hadn't I been more awake to notice Happy's approach?

On a farm like ours there was little time for inactive brooding, and I was grateful for the unrelenting pressure of routine demands. What also cheered me up a bit was the speed with which Patch improved as I intensified his training. I'd accepted by now that almost certainly Happy would never work again; walk, maybe, even run a little, but to expect more was simply to be unrealistic.

For the first three weeks or so after the accident she didn't attempt to stir in her box; and when she did, pathetically to crawl or shuffle outside to relieve herself, we had to lift her down the kitchen door step, and up again. Encouragingly her lacerations were healing, but the two legs most severely damaged made it as plain as commonsense she didn't stand a chance of functioning again as a working sheepdog. Not a hope in hell.

Whether Patch sensed this, or something like it, I can't, of course, be sure, but he seemed to take a quickened interest in his training. At any rate his progress was little short of incredible. The training programme I adopted for him was virtually identical to Happy's.

There were differences, inevitably, reflecting the personality and temperament of the two dogs, never mind the suddenly changed circumstances at the farm itself. But all this apart, Patch was, I soon discovered, ready for serious training. I should have realized by the way he eyed the hens and ducks at every opportunity; indeed, he eyed pretty well everything that moved, from tractor to cat to the unlikely new cockerel. In such matters he was just as playful as Happy at a comparable age, as playful and roguish, but unlike her he rarely concluded this eyeing of his two-legged friends of the farmyard by scattering them when they were least awake to his presence.

Having sharpened his understanding of the basic commands, I again brought in the ducks, all four this time, to help with his approach work. We had a spot of bother with his impetuosity to get to the ducks too directly, as with Happy, but unlike her he showed no preference for the left approach, performing from both sides eventually with equal competence.

From a remarkably early age he'd indicated his interest in the sheep, ears pricked whenever he saw them, often like a predator pulling on an invisible leash. What we still didn't know about was the degree of his courage. Eyeing hens and ducks for fun was one thing, coping with a wily ewe or surly ram was something else. We could only wait and see.

Happy's condition changed little. She was now able to limp from her box to answer the call of nature, even to negotiate the kitchen doorstep, but careful all the time to keep her most heavily bandaged leg and foot off the ground. Otherwise her pre-accident hectic life was replaced by barely more than waiting, a picture of hated redundancy. Naturally we all fussed her at every opportunity, and the children, desperate to offer comfort, even took her for a walk in a battered doll's pram, surely the final indignity for a farm sheepdog, but with our long absences all over the farm plus the children being at school I was well aware of her loneliness.

There was also, I realized, her possible misery at being deserted by me, for this is what it must have looked like to her, especially as she watched Patch increasingly often leaving the farmhouse in my company, occasionally, it's true, to be sent back, but progressively to remain with me for hours at a stretch.

Bill Wheel kept telling me that a dog as bright as Happy would understand. I wasn't convinced. The only thing of which I was certain was the look of anguish in her eyes; not the anguish of pain – that stage, thanks to the vet's skill and continuing concern, was soon left behind – but the anguish of helpless uselessness. Probably I'm projecting, at least partly, but each time I saw her that's how her haunted look struck me.

It didn't take much imagination to see from her point of view the utter transformation of her world. From being an indispensable and near omnipresent partner on the farm she was now ignored for most of the day, and thrown only occasional crumbs of comfort as we hurried to the next pressing job. When the children were home from school it wasn't so bad, but neither my wife nor I was rarely in the farmhouse for more than minutes at a time.

In this long emptiness, Happy's only company were our two domestic moggies whose initial quite enthusiastic tolerance of her hadn't survived their own noses being put out of joint by yet another competitor for our affection and notice. More and more they gave her the cold shoulder.

Patch was friendly enough, but with his growing pre-occupation with training, and decided preference for being out of doors, there was little time left during the day for his keeping Happy company. She must have been bewildered and wretched beyond description.

Another job during which Happy's absence brought her constantly to mind was shearing. Patch couldn't help at all to get the flock penned, and likewise did nothing to push the sheep on their rightful way as each was released to pasture after the clipping.

Shearing! I'm not surprised every farmer I know calls in a contract shearer. We tried to manage without one, but were soon ready to admit the sheep deserved better. Once more I turned to Bill for guidance.

Inevitably he knew just the man – a council worker in

the roads department! The old countryman laughed at my astonishment. This man, too, Bill explained, like his mate the factory worker, had been a farm labourer, in the bad old days when agricultural skills demanding years of training and experience were rewarded with a weekly pittance. It's better now, Bill smiled, leaving me in no doubt he meant the opposite; better, he added, but not good enough.

Anyhow, the council worker, roots deep in the soil, loving farm work but hating the long hours seven days a week, forget the derisory wages, was more than happy to engage in spare-time shearing, at a price, of course. Bill promised he'd fix it.

The man arrived on Saturday morning, shortly after first light. A couple of days before, he'd sent a message that he wanted the sheep penned and ready for an early start. Early! I hadn't even started the milking.

He set up his gear and drank coffee as our chain of human sheepdogs – hindered by Patch who was finally banished to the kitchen to keep Happy company – advanced first up the field and then back again this time behind the sheep. The whole episode was another ten minutes or so when the lament 'If only . . .' was again centred exclusively on our crippled dog.

At last the sheep were penned. The shearer stripped to the waist, grabbed and upended his first unsuspecting customer in one lightning movement, and switched on his electric cutters. Hour after hour he kept at it, bent double over the sheep, deftly working it from one position to another using its bottom as a pivot, removing the fleece in a single piece, sheer artistry, and casting it aside to be rolled and tied later as he grabbed the next in line. Merely watching, my back was killing me.

And the thought saddened me – how come this highly

skilled craftsman found it necessary to dig roads for a living? Doubtless digging or repairing roads also had its degree of expertise; but if ever a worker's real talent was being virtually buried by a traditional underestimation of agricultural craftsmanship here was a perfect example. What a waste, not only to our whole community but the man himself.

When he stopped for a mid-morning cup of tea brought to him by my wife, he told us he loved farm work generally but simply couldn't afford the luxury. Then was working for the council, I enquired, so much more financially rewarding? His smile left me in no doubt; and his basic working week, thirty-nine hours, was so much more reasonable for a family man.

Altogether it took him one whole week-end and a couple of evenings of the following week – after his day's work! – to complete the shearing. Of his four days with us, he stopped before dusk only once – when he ran out of sheep.

The denuded flock, I must say, looked most peculiar, like a different breed or animal, but in this sweltering weather they must have been grateful to be free of their coats.

Almost, in fact, as grateful as us. The local wool marketing board, having indiscriminately pulled out hand-fuls from our delivery to assess general quality, promised us an early cheque. But even this wasn't the most signific-ant outcome of the shearing. Very very occasionally, some things on a sheepfarm are more important than money! You find this hard to believe? Well, make up your own mind as you read.

Actually, the outcome of the shearing had two distinct elements or parts. The first involved Patch. I've men-tioned how his basic training was intensified, but of course he was too young to be much help with the sheep. There was no doubting his wish to run them (in contrast, you remember, to running after them), but this didn't compensate for his inexperience or guarantee that when testing situations arose he would be able to cope. Nevertheless I was delighted with his general progress.

On the final day of the shearing, the ewes almost finished, I collected our two rams from the meadow, not a dog in sight. No suggestion of awkwardness, they strolled past the farmhouse, through the farmyard, and into the makeshift pen by the shearer as though aware the whole point of the exercise was to rid them of their heavy coats.

As the last denuded ewe trotted away to join the grazing flock, he grabbed the nearer ram, which happened to be the younger and normally more docile, sat him upright between his legs, and switched on his shears.

Still fascinated by his skill and rate of work, I barely noticed the arrival of Patch, apart from feeling grateful he was content to watch from the other side of the farmyard gate. He peered through the bars, keeping well out of the way.

The senior ram was as submissive as the first, and within minutes the shearer unbent his back for the first time since starting the session. He cleaned his gear, washed at the cowshed tap, and climbed into his van, a broad smile on his face. I promised payment after calling at the bank the next day.

It was only as he revved away that I became aware of the senior ram's quiet determination to join the flock at the other end of the field; he was already half way there. Obviously the shearer, impatient to get away or more likely knowing that both rams were immediately to be returned to the meadow, hadn't bothered to pen the second. And as I set off to retrieve the wanderer I received my first inkling he was in no mood to sustain his uncharacteristic meekness.

I quickened my step. So did he. Exasperated, again wishing Happy was her old self, I yelled and threatened, the distance between us meanwhile getting no shorter. Vaguely I heard my wife calling, then insistently, and the next thing I knew Patch, the reason for her calls, flashed past me in a straight line for the ram. I screamed at him to lie down, LIE DOWN; but if he heard me at all, which I doubt, his single concern was the ram.

They reached the fence almost together. The pursued, openly contemptuous of this irritating whippersnapper, trotted alongside it, apparently wholly indifferent to the dog. Until he found himself restricted by the fence and a drinking trough, with nowhere to go but head on at the impertinence barring the way.

Not hesitating he charged. And for the first time I watched a ram seriously take on a sheepdog. Maybe it happens often with young and inexperienced dogs, but never before as far as we were concerned.

The encounter lasted for an eternity of seconds. Patch was bundled aside by the sheer weight of the rampaging ram, knocked flying by the impact. His only response was to pick himself up and go for the ram. I wouldn't have believed it. This comparatively small animal, not a hint of wanting to back off or scarper, set about this belligerent affront to his dignity as though his life or at least his self-respect depended upon it. Perhaps it did.

In any case, Patch rapidly turned the tables by snapping at the ram's nose, and further encouraged complete capitulation by repeatedly nipping a massive retreating backside. Watching, heart in my mouth, there suddenly flashed to my mind the old shepherd's admonition shortly

174

after we'd observed Happy operating with his bull – never underestimate your dog!

LIE DOWN, I shouted at Patch as he chased the ram to the other end of the field; and then chased him back again. Talk about pandemonium! By the time the dog was under some sort of control the ram was almost appealing to me for protection. Which brings me – almost – to the second significant part of the shearing's outcome. I say *almost* because first I had to collect both rams and set them on their way to the meadow. With Patch now walking to heel we pushed them through the farmyard and once more past the farmhouse into a field adjacent to the meadow.

All went well until the rams found irresistible a gate that should have been closed at the entrance to our vegetable garden. Even on a well regulated sheep farm these things do happen!

In a trice their unintentional vandalism started – tearing up, breaking down, bolting from one part of the garden to another, utterly to no purpose. And here's the amazing thing. Patch stayed with me, clearly longing to give chase but obedient to my command, a veritable extreme contrast to the tearaway of the previous five minutes. This wasn't all.

More incredible still, like an apparition, through the kitchen door hobbled Happy on three legs. Her direction was never in doubt. Straight to the vegetable garden. Once inside she made her favoured approach from the left. One ram joined the other as they shot through the strawberries into a far corner of the garden opposite the exit.

Happy, ears pricked, undercarriage almost touching the ground, inched forward, gently working the rams past the potatoes and onions, round the patch of runner beans, and finally behind the greenhouse. They shot through the gate, followed by Happy on *four* legs. I couldn't believe it.

Having satisfied herself the rams were on their rightful way, she made no attempt to follow them, but, tail wagging, looking decidedly pleased with herself, she came across to join us, her most heavily bandaged leg once more off the ground.

I didn't know whether to laugh or cry. In the event I think I did both. And even now I still feel the excitement of those moments, among the most unforgettable of my life. This dog which at one time looked like never being able to walk again was back in harness, admittedly only a shadow of her former speedy self, but surely with already enough of her old competence to justify my unbounded optimism.

Never mind the rams, let them enjoy the freedom of the entire farm if needs be, I rushed to the farmhouse to break the news to the family. It was, as we understood it, a miracle. The impossible had happened. The only one not surprised was perhaps the happiest. I won't say she spent the next excited minutes repeating 'I told you so', but the rest of us were left in no doubt that this was what she meant.

Eventually all three of us – Happy, Patch and I – completed the placing of the rams, though in fact they almost did the job for us. What a difference the mere presence of Happy appeared to make! That, in any case, was my conclusion as, still bubbling with this totally unexpected development, I closed the gate of the meadow.

Happy herself, I swear, knew she'd done something akin to walking on water. Like a shy prima donna, she nuzzled her nose into my lap as I rubbed her behind the ears, all the time whispering sweet nothings into them. What a sheepdog! Even Patch seemed to understand. I've mentioned before the danger of people projecting their own feelings on to animals, most of all their pets, but it did honestly seem to me that Patch shared our jubilation at what was, after all, tantamount to Happy's return from the dead. I tell you, we returned to the farmhouse like a trio of happy conspirators, as though between us we'd defied the very laws of the natural world.

Predictably Bill Wheel played it cool; couldn't understand what all the fuss was about. He'd known all along the dog would recover. As for Fred the cat lover, he was too impatient to tell me the latest exploits of his ferals to indicate what he thought about the miracle I claimed. The rat, he began, was this long . . . It was like listening to a recording. And Fred doesn't believe in all this projection of feelings nonsense. He just knows – with the unerring certainty of an Old Moore's Almanac – what his cats are thinking and feeling. Nor does he doubt their mystical powers to communicate to him alone their every opinion and change of mood. Whatever I think about Fred's love affair with his cats, I can't help but admire his total devotion. My only regret is his unyielding obsession, even when all I want is to tell him about the resurrection from the dead of a superb sheepdog.

The vet was something else. He called to take a sample of the calves' blood. In answer to my call Happy came bouncing from the Tyler barn, still on three legs but almost as fast as if on four. He examined the scars on the three, removed the bandage to inspect the fourth, seemed unsure, appeared to hesitate; then glowed with pleasure at the results of his handiwork. 'Makes it all worth while,' he laughed. And I knew exactly what he meant.

* * *

177

I wish the same could be said for something that happened the next day. I'd just finished washing the car, a chore I try to forget for weeks at a time, when hundreds of starlings, like a circling black cloud, actually turned the bright afternoon into twilight.

They dived, swooped, climbed, squawked; and then – as though controlled by clockwork – indulged mightily in corporate defecation. Like slimy rain.

Despairingly I looked at the recently white-washed walls of the cowshed.

Too late my wife cleared her wash line.

As for the car . . .

Having made their mark the starlings disappeared as quickly as they'd come. You might say it was all over in a minute. All over! I never knew starlings were inclined to communal turn-outs. Or was it quite fortuitously the co-ordinated result of something they'd eaten? I shall never know.

What I can't doubt is the special relationship starlings appear to have with sheep. Throughout the summer there are few occasions when I look at the flock without seeing these beautiful but pugnacious birds either riding on the sheep's back possibly searching for parasite pickings from their wool or nipping between their legs though for what purpose I'm never sure. Bill Wheel reckons they hide under sheep from their predators – when a member of the hawk family is in the vicinity! He could be right, usually is in such matters, but I suspect a more likely explanation is their continued search for food. As much as I detest their aptitude for roughing up smaller birds at least whenever food is in the offing I can't help but like their fierce independence and of course the loveliness of their plumage. If there were not so many of them, and their behaviour was less belligerent, I imagine their colouring would be appreciated almost as much as a kingfisher's. As it is, they seem doomed to suffer human hostility.

And I know all about human hostility. Or you might say I had a spot of bother with our village publican's wife. To be fair, she was entitled to be upset; but in extenuation the nature of her problem, never mind ours, simply revealed itself too late.

We have a friend in the village who keeps a few sheep as a sideline on a bit of land not far from the pub. Our involvement started because we have a marvellous neighbour whose numerous kindnesses include allowing us to push our flock through his sheep dip; and he didn't hesitate when I requested that this same facility be extended to our friend's sheep, only twenty-five or so.

There was only one snag. Whereas our sheep were only three fields away from the dip, our friend's were almost a couple of miles, and neither of us had adequate transport. Not to worry, logic being the soul of invention, we finally decided, all things considered, the sheep would have to walk.

We fixed the day, and carefully laid our plans. In fairness to all impatient drivers using our lonely roads we'd make an early start and have the sheep back in their own pasture before most people were up and about. Long before first light I arrived with Happy, but our friend and his dog were already waiting. Incidentally, why no Patch? He simply wasn't skilful enough to be trusted on the public highway. Not yet. Not with a job new to all of us.

Taking no chances Happy and I went ahead, leaving our friend and his dog to keep things moving from behind. It worked like a dream. The only suggestion of trouble was when one of the lambs began to cough, nothing unusual in itself, but this sounded bad, possibly terminal without caution. Our friend decided to return the lamb to his smallholding while Happy and I pushed on with the sheep, I still leading, the dog now at the rear.

No problems. The morning was glorious, comfortably warm yet with the slightest nip in the air to heighten pleasure. At this rate, I thought, we'll soon be settling down to the farmhouse breakfast my wife had promised by way of celebration.

Then the hesitation of a leading sheep brought to my attention a barely open garden gate standing back on the opposite side of the road. Now you already know from our rams and the vegetable garden episode that sheep can be unbelievably stupid. And this stupidity is never more pronounced than when they happen upon a gate that should be closed, most of all such a gate with lovingly attended lawns behind it.

With this in mind I bolted across the road and managed to close the gate just in time. But not before some of the sheep had gone ahead. Understandably my panic to cut them off drove them on – straight toward the pub's prize-winning gardens.

Sensing my desperation Happy, frantic to help but still restricted by her tender feet, began to bark, further scattering the sheep as they poured into the gardens, and, charging everywhere, proceeded to churn up, break down, flatten, and – most noticeable of all on the immaculate lawns – massively fertilize the lot.

At which indelicate moment the publican's wife stuck her head through an upstairs window. Her mouth fell open. Horror stole across her face. She began to gesticulate wildly. And shout. Mercifully, above the baaing and barking and general chaos, I couldn't make out what she was trying to communicate; but one thing was crystal clear – if looks could kill I wouldn't be re-living the nightmare.

Eventually, after an eternity of minutes, the upstairs window still open, the face through it now gazing in stunned silence, our friend and his dog returned, and we managed to set the sheep on their orderly way. By comparison there were no further mishaps. True, our friend's dog fell into the dip; and a strong-willed ewe, defeating our efforts to prevent her clambering out too quickly, spitefully objected to being picked off for a second dipping. But, as I say, by comparison it was a piece of cake. All that remained was to get the sheep back to pasture, this time past the pub.

Periodically we drove them into a gateway to clear the road, but drivers late for work can be hard to please, though to be fair most seemed charmed by the sight of a shepherd and his dog leading a flock, and a similar devoted partnership coming on behind, a pastoral scene rare these days even in our farming area.

My main concern remained, of course, the publican's wife. And perhaps it would have helped if before knocking on the door I had taken time to change out of my sodden trousers stinking of sheep dip and other offences. She called her husband. We talked. I explained. My apology was heartfelt. And she almost managed a smile. Almost.

It must have been all that free fertilizer.

Happily the dipping of our own flock proved much less hectic. Happy and Patch approached the flock from opposite sides and gently herded them through three fields to the dip itself behind our neighbour's barn, accessible enough from our farm to suggest he'd put it there for our convenience.

As with every time she was now involved with the sheep, Happy's fourth leg came down, forgotten in her zest for work. Watching her hopping about on three, and then take off on all four to function with her old enthusiasm, I found it hard to believe that so recently she had seemed doomed to be a cripple for the rest of her life.

The sheep were penned, no aggro, with a single-file exit adjacent to the dip. One or two obligingly jumped or fell in, but the majority needed the persuasion of a push, while a few really awkward customers dared us to overcome their resolve to avoid the plunge. But once in, the frantic concern of the whole lot was to get out, their only hindrance being our determination through a ducking pole to ensure a thorough soaking.

By late morning the last of our flock was shaking itself dry and – smelling of hygienic cleanliness – heading for home. I sent them on with the dogs, and stood chatting to our neighbour's son, shepherd to his father's considerable flock but on this occasion intent on putting a dozen sheep or so including three rams through the dip.

The rams, each a magnificent specimen, appeared as docile as the rest as they went through or at least in, becoming obstreperous only as they fought the ducking pole to reach the sloping exit. This achieved they shook themselves dry, spraying the antibiotic too close for our comfort, and benignly re-joined the sheep. The shepherd and I continued to chat, barely noticing as one of his men started to release them to pasture. Only a bone crunching thud caused us to look over.

Two rams facing each other in combat!

This, as you know, was nothing unusual; our own rams joined in the favoured pastime notably just before tupping. What made this encounter different was the gross unevenness of the contest. One ram, a Kent, was a veritable colossus, almost twice the size of the other, a black face Suffolk. Yet the pair of them were indistinguishable in bellicosity. Never mind the first almighty collision, they hurriedly stood back for a second murderous or suicidal charge. Thud!

By now the shepherd and his dog were rushing to rescue the contestants from each other, but the Suffolk no less than the bulldozer Kent appeared for a moment to be prepared to take on the dog in his frenzy to continue the lopsided fight. Are rams stupid or naturally incapable – like Siamese male fighting fish – of not taking each other on, even when one is likely to be pulverized by the sheer bulk of the other?

On second thoughts, perhaps size or weight isn't the main factor, for the dog quickly asserted his authority, chasing the rams apart, and seeing them to their separate enclosures. Nevertheless, it was apparent from the way the contestants continued to glare at each other that neither could wait to renew the battle.

This whole question of the latent viciousness in otherwise friendly animals never ceases to astonish me. Whether rams or Jack Russells or Fred's feral cats, to name but three, are involved, I watch and wonder. One lunch time, for instance, I was leaning over a gate eyeing half a dozen sheep with a possible purchase in mind. Out of the hedge bordering Fred's allotment hopped a rabbit, not hanging about, followed shortly afterwards by a cat which surprisingly veered to the left alongside the hedge, giving the impression its disinterest in the rabbit was final.

Somehow quickly aware it was no longer being chased, the rabbit sat watching the cat sloping away, evidently in no doubt that even disappearing cats weren't to be trusted. For another minute or so, ears pricked, everything about it the very embodiment of caution, suspicion, it stared after the now invisible cat before feeding and hopping a little nearer the hedge, presumably the way home.

The owner of the sheep and his dog approached from the other side of the field parallel to the hedge, finally leaving the rabbit no option but to escape through it. But even before it reached this desirable cover, out sprang the waiting cat, that dear silky creature which barely seconds before had strolled away from the rabbit looking as though butter wouldn't melt in its mouth.

It was, as they say in pugilist circles, a no contest. The rabbit didn't have a chance. There wasn't time for any fur to fly. The snarling spitting feline ended proceedings almost before they started, and nearly instantaneously reverted to the furry little creature Fred never tires of eulogizing for its remarkable friendliness despite its half-wild way of life and habitat.

In any case, wholly domesticated cats – certainly in our part of the world – are equally capable of this bloody ferocity. I know. One of our farmhouse moggies, a spayed tom, accustomed to ample rations twice a day, usually too lazy to bestir himself for anything but another cuddle, living like an aristocrat never mind his dubious lineage, is nevertheless capable of lethal hunting. And why not? He's only being himself, his basic or primitive self. The thing that offends me is the way he plays with some of his smaller victims before dispatching them. I interfere when I can, which both Bill and Fred condemn as a townee diabolical liberty; unforgivably unfair to the cat!

My problem is to differentiate between sensitive realism and sentimentality, the precise point where one ends and the other begins. To be utterly unfeeling is, it seems to me, impossible or indecent (evidence of being a moron) whereas to be too emotional is fanaticism or self-indulgence (evidence of a maladjusted personality). Our family reaction to what happened to one of our sock lambs shortly after our spot of bother with the publican's wife probably illustrates the problem perfectly.

A cattle transporter pulled into the farmyard. The children in particular watched disconsolately. I helped load the lambs for market, both Happy and Patch in attendance, and slipped the safety catch into position. With a cheery wave the driver pulled away.

Silently the children got into the car for school, their accusing eyes focused exclusively on me.

Murderer!

I should make clear it wasn't the first time the transporter had called, its purpose clearly understood and taken for granted. The fuss on this occasion originated weeks before, shortly after I'd battled unsuccessfully to save the life of a day-old lamb. Feeling wretched, surprised and to be honest a little annoyed that such an inevitable part of even a good lambing season should still hurt so much, I picked up the tiny corpse and made for the farm workshop.

Probably to counter my mood my eyes searched for one of my favourite ewes. As one of our very first sheep she'd played no small part in teaching an unlikely candidate like me the basics of sheep farming. Into the bargain she'd provided the biggest surprise of the entire lambing.

First of all I thought she'd had twins. A moment later I looked again, unbelievingly. The twins were now triplets. Forget the desirability of being a hardened shepherd, indifferent to the ups no less than the downs, I nipped to the farmhouse to call my wife. By the time we both returned, a couple of minutes, we found it necessary to take a longer, harder look.

Incredible.

Impossible.

'Quads,' she whispered.

Now most of our sheep are Kents, sometimes called Romneys, a breed noted for meat and quality of wool rather than reproductive capacity. True, twins are not all that unusual; but triplets are rare, quads almost unheard of! Even our neighbours, farming families for generations, said four was unique in their experience.

Naturally my immediate concern was whether the ewe had enough milk. Within twenty-four hours it was clear she could best cope with no more than two. So what about the other two? Merely to ask with a dead lamb in my arms was to remember a bereaved ewe with an udder full of milk going to waste.

Her immediate reaction was to sniff the smaller of the two lambs, sniff again just to be sure, and show her disinterest. But with Happy crouched in the pen, not too near but near enough to concentrate the mind, she made no attempt to butt the lamb aside. As usual I held her while the lamb suckled, and left the three of them to sort out their differences. They did. Eventually. Which left the fourth lamb.

Clearly the only solution was the bottle, initially a demanding task but in this special case – one of quads! – one cheerily undertaken by the children. And with so much loving attention, extra rations aside, the lamb grew fat and big, a real beauty. The only doubt that flitted across my mind was when the children, treating the lamb like a pet, gave it a name. Frank – for a female lamb!

What inspired this unlikely choice I couldn't imagine, but I knew beyond doubt that trouble was ahead.

Frank ignored the rest of the flock, preferring the company of two-legged sheep. Seeing the children anywhere on the farm he (she) rushed over demanding their undivided attention for a cuddle. Their devotion never turned him (her) away disappointed. And, of course, long after Frank was ready for market the children's fierce protective custody kept the indulged creature out of harm's way.

The problem was – I knew and so did they – the moment of truth could not be postponed indefinitely. We were running a sheep farm, not an animal sanctuary.

So now you understand why the departure of this particular transporter was something of a family crisis. The children, never mind the rest of us, were in mourning for a week. Yes, only a week, such was their resilience coupled to the excitement of a muscovy duck emerging at the head of a crocodile of impatiently awaited ducklings, but even now, whenever the irreplaceable Frank is mentioned, I get the firm impression I'm not entirely forgiven.

What decidedly helped toward a reconciliation was my belated agreement to a request from the children about a money raising project at school. For quite a time I was adamantly against, not the end but the means. Good cause or not, I couldn't see why either Happy or Patch should be subjected to the indignity of taking part in a pets' show and obedience competition. They were working sheepdogs, not a spectacle to be gawped at by people who didn't know the difference between purposeful obedience and puppetry.

My wife told me not to be so pompous. The children insisted the competition, open to pets of all shapes and sizes, was for real; and in any case the main idea was to have fun as well as raise money.

I ruled Happy out straightaway. Apart from her accident, her high degree of training and skill gave her an unfair advantage. Or so my pride wanted to believe. The children readily conceded. But what, they retaliated, about Patch? He wasn't consistently obedient; not yet. I asked whether they'd noticed his vast improvement since Happy's accident? They had, but he still wasn't obedient all the time. In that case, I asked, why bother entering him for the competition? Because, they chorused, there was no other choice. The angora rabbits? A duck? A hen? They told me not to be silly.

In the end I reluctantly agreed on one condition. They find out exactly what was required, and prepare Patch accordingly themselves. They explained that not knowing beforehand was itself part of the test. It was also part of the fun.

I hate to admit it, but my reluctance was at least partially a reflection of my fear that Patch would make a fool of himself. And me. In the event, I needn't have worried, for wholly the wrong reason.

I'd never seen such a collection of pets! Forget the countless dogs, cats, and hamsters, there was a pony, a donkey, a duck, a piglet, a lamb, a goldfish, a parrot, a pigeon, in fact, a veritable Noah's Ark. And as for the so-called obedience test, it barely got underway. The judges were too preoccupied awarding prizes for the most unusual pet, the biggest, the smallest, the most appealing eyes, the loveliest coat, the best behaved, and so on ad infinitum until pretty well everybody received an award. If they didn't the judges weren't to blame.

Patch returned home understandably protesting about a 'winner' rosette attached to his collar. To achieve this distinction he was required to stand alone and wait until called by one of the children some ten strides away. Even the donkey was among the winners. Incidentally, the mother of the girl who entered him and did the calling told me donkeys are unjustifiably maligned as stupid. They learn quickly, she said. The primary requirement is kindness. True or false, the occasion itself was a huge financial success; and by the end had turned into quite a village festival.

Nevertheless, the next morning brought my wife and me, if not the children, down to earth with a bang. Sending Frank to market had been hard. Culling the flock proved to be much harder. I've mentioned how a shepherd comes to know his flock individually – idiosyncrasies, temperament, mannerisms, gait, face, ears, any number of distinguishing indicators. This applies equally to every animal on the farm, but by the very nature of things to some more equally than others. The self-appointed leader of our flock was a case in point.

This lovable rogue was a member of our first tiny flock, and despite subsequent additions her preeminence was never seriously in doubt. Likely successors were put in their place, no real argument, leaving her authority wholly undisputed.

Even Happy approached her with far-sighted circumspection, knowing she must never be taken for granted. Too often she toed the line only after a display of fierce independence. Come to think of it, I've already mentioned how she alone really resisted being separated from her lamb, sending one of the children flying, and later that night finding a way through a couple of fences for reunion celebrations.

This endearing bloody-mindedness naturally made her

a problem to handle. While the vast majority of the sheep surrendered to foot inspections, hoof trimming, douching, injections or whatever, she persisted in adding zest to life, keeping us on edge as to which way she would jump. What we would have done without Happy's matching determination I can't or won't imagine.

On one occasion she fought, I shall never forget, like a cornered bull to avoid the douching instrument being placed in her mouth long enough for the antibiotic to be squirted down her throat. Yet paradoxically her awkwardness added to her appeal. She was a character, not exactly a wolf in sheep's coating but with enough similar tendencies to lead the unwary up the garden path. We thought the world of her.

So when a dental inspection confirmed our worst fears we were saddened but nonetheless undeterred – a sheep, leader of the flock or not, that can't eat has no place on a farm. I know there's serious talk of fixing up sheep with dentures – and I'm not joking – but it won't happen yet awhile, if at all, and in the interim, once a sheep's teeth decay or fall out through ageing, nothing can be done. Nothing.

Which explains why the morning after the pets' show and obedience test, my wife and I left the farmhouse with the two dogs feeling much less enthusiastic than either. The children were with us, utterly unconcerned about the pending arrival of the cattle transporter. Sending Frank to market was terrible, culling the flock with the same end in view was apparently entirely different. They were still laughing among themselves about the delights of the previous afternoon.

We penned the entire flock in no time, but not before noticing a couple of ewes limping, probably early sign of footrot. Putting them aside for closer inspection later, we pushed the rest through the separating race to complete the culling. Soon the ten unfortunates were segregated and penned in the farmyard. The children ran off to play, not a care in the world. I, on the other hand, each time I went near these old friends, felt wretched, confident they knew for sure what was going on.

I came to believe that animals somehow smell fear and death in certain situations when I delivered four of our first litter of piglets to the slaughterhouse. They were about four months old, as lively as such young pigs usually are, until we reached the abattoir. The transformation was pathetic. Let there be no misunderstanding: like all meat growers, let alone meat eaters, I'm grateful to the workers in such places. My limited experience tells me they are both humane themselves and use humane methods. But this doesn't alter the fact that the animals appear to pick up with growing terror the imminence of execution.

Anyway, trying to put the culled faithfuls out of my mind, I concentrated upon the footrot suspects. This common disease among sheep – another that defies all precautions and care – starts as a mild inflammation between the claws, and develops quickly into a split between the skin and the hoofhorn, accompanied by a characteristic stinking discharge. Absolutely foul. The treatment, usually straightforward enough, is a question unfortunately of being cruel to be kind.

Essentially the affected area is fully exposed before an antiseptic is applied, and this involves the use of both secateurs and a scalpel. I'd attended to the first ewe and was about to start on the second when the driver of the transporter pulled into the farmyard. He waved a greeting, was typically amiable, but made it crystal clear he didn't want to hang about.

The transporter was backed up to the pen so that when

he unlatched and lowered the walk-up the sheep were no more than half-a-dozen strides away. Too casually I grabbed the nearest and set it on its way, momentarily leaving the exit from the pen unattended. In a flash the erstwhile leader of the flock was through, naturally taking the rest with her, all of them sufficiently crazed with fear to dart past the dogs.

Patch leaped after the toothless wonder which, trapped between the dog and a fence, feigned a charge, thought better of it, but still somehow broke out to disappear into the Tyler barn. Meanwhile Happy, showing no signs of being tender footed, rounded up the other less determined escapees. Immediately they were safely loaded we left her guarding the exit, and went in search of Patch.

He and his quarry were panting hard at each other, the distance between them no more than a stride but preserved by mutual caution and respect. I wouldn't go so far as to say Patch was intimidated, but he seemed less than keen to resolve the deadlock. Even so, his presence was enough to concentrate the old sheep's mind, making it relatively easy for me to grab a hock and bundle her into the transporter. Laughing his head off, the driver revved the engine and was away.

Ironically the excitement helped to lessen the pain of parting. Almost cheerfully I walked to the farmhouse for a quick coffee, Happy as usual to heel, with I presumed Patch in tow. In front of the first log fire of the autumn my wife was spinning wool, a skill she learned from a self-sufficiency fanatic in the next village. Watching not only fascinates me but tugs at something basic to my make-up. Whether the appeal is the smell of the wool, never washed before the spinning, or the sound of the wheel I'm not sure, but few things give me greater pleasure notably on long winter evenings.

My wife joined me for a coffee, laughingly I told her of the pandemonium of the previous five minutes, and in next to no time I was on my way back to the farmyard.

Patch was lying near the gate, apparently lifeless, nothing remotely to suggest why. My wife cradled him in her arms as I drove to the vet's where the kindly man asked me questions I couldn't answer, and looked increasingly baffled. Less than forty minutes before this brave little dog was facing the rampaging ewe in the barn. Now he was barely alive. Yes, but why? WHY? The whole thing was senseless. Bizarre.

The vet suggested we leave Patch at the surgery, and promised he'd phone immediately if anything developed. Less than two hours later, even before I picked up the phone, I knew.

Patch was dead.

In trying to comfort each other and the children, my wife and I racked our brains to fathom the mystery. There wasn't a clue on the farm, not a mark on the dog. One moment he was bouncing with vitality, the next unconscious. Now dead. The vet agreed to carry out a post-mortem. We simply had to have an explanation. But his findings, though conclusive, didn't help one little bit.

Patch, his throat dry after chasing and cornering the ewe in the barn, apparently quenched his thirst from the first bowl he saw – dregs of the footrot antiseptic. In being called away by the arrival of the transporter, I'd left it lying about; but in any case it never crossed my mind there was danger. Happy must have passed the stuff times without number both before and after Patch's arrival, and never once showed the slightest interest. Surely Patch was bright enough to know the difference between water and burning formalin!

Such arguments or rationalizations or excuses were, of

course, utterly pointless, a waste of time. We were devastated. Happy's accident was shattering enough, but nothing like this. The gloom followed us everywhere; and even now, after much of the self-recrimination and despair and sickness of heart have relented, refuses to lift entirely.

Dear old Patch.

It was, I think, our growing longing for another dog to fill the unfillable that prompted me to seek a suitable mate for Happy the next time she came into season, about four months later. My chronic guilt no less than all our fond memories of Patch convinced us that he was irreplaceable, a sheepdog in a million, destined but for my carelessness to outstrip even Happy as a working partner on the farm. In my more objective moments I had to admit that he never really had time to indicate the true measure of his potential. Whether he would have gone on to fulfil our most optimistic expectations must remain an open question. What we never doubted was that a puppy of Happy's was most likely to fill the void in our affections. Sentimentality rearing its head again?

If Bill Wheel thought so he didn't say. On the contrary, his first reaction was to offer to approach his brother for the use of one of his studs, guarantee of quality, a request, incidentally, readily granted. What somewhat dented my enthusiasm was the proposed agreement – first choice of the litter by the stud's owner. I knew this was thought to be fair, as well as a fairly common agreement, but I declined for another reason altogether.

From the moment I'd watched Patch's parents at work, I'd secretly hoped that one day his father would sire Happy's whelps. Furthermore my wife and I had been in regular touch with the farmer and his former nursing-sister wife through the common interest of their teenage son and our eldest daughter in more than angora rabbits. So a brief phone call finalized arrangements, plus an invitation to the entire family to take Happy over and leave her overnight.

Not to worry, our genial host assured us, Ben will know what to do. He did. For half-way through a delightful meal a report came to hand that the dogs were already locked and turned, hopeful sign of a fruitful outcome. The one requirement now was patience.

Happy herself didn't appear to notice the progressive signs of her being in whelp, and made no concessions to her work load, even when her undercarriage of swelling teats at least looked cumbersome. As usual she greeted my appearance in the kitchen at first light, stood wagging her tail in eagerness to be off as I sipped a life-rallying coffee, and simply shot through the garden gate on our way to milking.

A fortnight or so before her whelps were due, she made a puzzling adaptation to her long-standing habit of settling in a corner of the tractor cab whenever I climbed aboard. Bearing in mind her swinging undercarriage at every movement, I wasn't a bit surprised the first time she didn't take her customary place, my assumption being she was finally prepared to take life a little easier. Time to put her feet up in either the Tyler barn or the farmhouse kitchen! She did neither.

As I pulled away with supplementary winter feed for the sheep, Happy gently trotted behind, and followed me all over the farm. Periodically she rested, but never for more than a few minutes before returning to another bout of jogging. Once or twice I started to lift her into the cab, but quickly realized this was contrary to her wishes. Apparently it wasn't that she couldn't leap into the cab of her own volition. She preferred to walk or rather gently trot – sometimes, allowing for the breaks, for hours at a time.

Was this, I wondered, some sort of pre-natal exercise for an easier delivery? I shall never know. Even Bill and his brother, a vastly experienced breeder, had never come across such behaviour before. Their reaction was to leave well alone – the dog knew best. I agreed, sort of. But that swinging undercarriage of swelling teats did bother me at times.

A greater surprise still started not long after the mating and continued beyond the whelping itself. The first time it happened my wife was nonplussed. She answered the phone, and the caller wanted to know whether he could put his name down for one of Happy's puppies? My wife struggled for words: But we're not even sure she's taken; and anyhow, she caught her breath, how in the world do you know about Happy's whelping at all? Oh, I heard it on the grapevine, the caller laughed, a reference, we subsequently learned, to Bill.

Within the next few weeks, again because of the grapevine, we received three similar calls, and very soon realized that if only a portion of our grapevine callers were not to be disappointed Happy was required to produce an inordinate number of puppies.

With such a demand, we were resolved that any puppy we sold should go to a working situation, best guarantee of happiness, we believed, for a sheepdog. And this wasn't the only criterion. My wife, in charge of such transactions from the start, positively interrogated prospective customers, determined to satisfy herself that apart from being wanted to be trained as working partners the puppies would also be assured of good homes. Sad to say, we'd seen evidence that loyal hard-working sheep-dogs are not always appreciated. In other words, that some owners, happily very rare, do not recognize the difference between discipline and cruelty.

As things worked out, all the puppies but one went to farmers we knew or knew about through friends. The exception resulted from another grapevine call, from the girl with a face like a rosy apple, third-prize winner at the nursery novice trials. 'I don't know whether you remember me,' she said, 'you know, the supermarket cashier; we met . . .' And went on to tell a sad tale of the death of her dog in a car accident. 'If your puppies,' she completely won our hearts, 'are anything like Happy, I couldn't wish for a nicer replacement.'

The whelping itself seemed to be as easy as shelling peas, almost like a farrowing, for piglets tend to plop out so quickly the next one is missed if you blink. Happy chose to work until virtually the last moment. One morning early we were penning the flock for hoof inspection and trimming; her water broke, and she nipped away to an enlarged box by the kitchen stove to bring forth. By the time I knocked off for lunch she was suckling seven beautiful replicas of herself, five of them bitches.

The only time she appealed for help was when they outgrew the limited space in the kitchen. Until then it was wonderful fun for the family, but finally a danger underfoot to life and limb, not least for the puppies. So we transferred them to our ancient barn, part of it wholly draught proof, surrounding their snug bedding with bales of sweet-smelling hay.

Happy was a wonderful mother, but still persisted in not allowing her maternal preoccupations to hinder her working commitments. The first few days after the whelping I left the farmhouse expecting her to remain with her puppies, but invariably she walked to heel, and was always available as need arose. Periodically she slipped away to check their well-being, otherwise I barely noticed any difference in her constant companionship. Even after her accommodation was temporarily transferred to the barn, sure as anything, as soon as I set out for any part of the farm, she was quietly walking to heel, ears pricked, eyes alert, her whole being the embodiment of eagerness.

Watching her work the sheep, choose a lull to attend to her whelps, respond to my commands or use her own initiative in correcting either an obstreperous ewe or an oversight on my part, I found it difficult to believe she was the same dog I had carried to the vet with her legs cut to ribbons. Indeed, seeing her now, the ugly scars themselves barely visible unless you look hard, I wonder at her recovery. Of course we have the vet to thank for much. Of course nature herself is a wonderful healer. But none of this alters the fact that Happy's complete restoration was largely a matter of character. Her own indomitable spirit.

With such a mum, naturally the puppies thrived. And then we had the less than straightforward task of sorting out the placings of the available five. Five? Well, we'd promised one to the over-sized rosy apple; and then there was Patch's replacement! I was glad, as I say, to leave the entire fraught exercise to my wife. To adapt a biblical phrase, what were five among so many? Someone or two or three were bound to be disappointed, all of them suitable customers by my wife's stringent criteria of selection. Honesty alone compels me to confess that the quality of the whelps' mother was not the primary reason behind this excessive clamour. The reputation of the father and the history of some of the other puppies he'd sired contributed.

The one we kept to replace Patch really nominated himself. I subjected the lot to the usual tests – clapping my hands to see whether and how they scarpered, picking up each of them to get the feel of their bodily weight, something different from merely finding out which of them weighed most, looking for the aliveness in their eyes, their initiative in play, their inventiveness in climbing the Everest walls of their enclosure in the barn, plus the shape of the head and their general body structure. But at the end of the day, remembering that Happy herself had failed some of these reputed essentials of quality, we knew that the outcome of our choice was in the lap of the gods. Not, however, the choice itself.

Almost from the first, one in particular caught our eye. He was perky, cheeky, full of ingenuity at getting up to mischief, incapable of staying within the protective bales of hay, intended for warmth and safety barriers against tractors and the like in the farmyard, and utterly tenacious until triumphant.

Such spirit was sometimes not without price – like a thud as he fell or leaped to freedom from the heights of the intended prison walls, and what looked like a clip round the ears from his exasperated mum as he tried to plug in to an already occupied teat, and further his aptitude for fighting – playfully? – two or three of his kith and kin at once; all good fun, no doubt, but irrepressible self-assertiveness nonetheless. And just as he chose himself, so his name chose him.

Patch.

It wasn't important that his coat of black and white didn't remotely justify the choice. The reasons behind it were twofold, one unashamedly sentimental. We wanted to perpetuate the memory of a brave little dog; and also give expression to our hope that his replacement would somehow hide the fact of his absence. Foolish and unfair.

But it worked out all right. Though bearing a name that evoked for us, me especially, exaggerated expectations of near perfection, the newcomer from the onset was a personality in his own right, anything but a shadow of his beloved predecessor. In no time we stopped comparing the two, and to be honest found ourselves hardly thinking of the original Patch at all, not, needless to say, because he held any less significant a place in our affections but simply because the vacuum he left had been finally so completely filled.

There is, beyond doubt, something indefinable about the relationship between a shepherd and his dog. Essentially they are a team, mutually dependent, finding rare satisfaction from being together, working together, achieving together. A shepherd without his dog isn't merely handicapped. The very quality of his life is affected.

In partnership with Happy I frequently glimpse how primitive man must have felt as he hunted. For I become the pack leader, accepted by the dog as such, and use her to drive the quarry (the sheep) the way I want them to go. Or come. The link between us is an interchange of affection, respect and enjoyment, never fear, unless it be the fear of disappointing each other.

A sheepdog is, of course, quite capable of letting the shepherd down, but the more likely outcome, I reckon, happens the other way. Why? Because the shepherd, exposed to being worried about a whole range of concerns not immediately related to the task in hand, is liable to relieve his feelings of impatience and irritation by taking it out on the dog. Alas, I know!

Don't misunderstand. There must be firm discipline,

and not the slightest doubt that the shepherd or pack leader is in charge, but unless the working relationship remains one of pleasure on both sides it degenerates into little more than snarling tolerance.

The relationship between a shepherd and his dog represents something fundamentally different from one involving a highly trained pet. The working sheepdog *is* a pet, usually of the shepherd's doting family as well as himself, but the link between the two primary members of the partnership is, I think, unique, almost spiritual. Merely to write that makes me inwardly squirm, most of all with an image of down-to-earth Bill Wheel peering over my shoulder, yet no matter how seemingly extravagant and nebulous I still believe that some such word is required.

Talk to any shepherd with a happy dog, meaning a Happy sort of dog, and you'll know what I'm trying to say. Watch the pair of them working the flock or tramping pasture, the dog invariably to heel, and you'll understand. Hear the shepherd thinking aloud during long lonely hours of lambing, his dog always wide awake, quick to anticipate, sensitive to danger, never complaining, and you'll begin to appreciate the nature of the bond between them.

It *is* spiritual, a communion of minds, of souls (for want of a better word) – that essential something that makes the character of the dog no less than of the shepherd far more than a sum total of external identification. Sentimental claptrap? I stand by every word, only regretting that I can't be more specific or explicit.

All of which implies that the average working sheepdog, by the very nature of its life-style, is a one man or one woman dog. But this doesn't mean, as I've already underlined, that the dog isn't capable of working with other than the one with whom the special relationship has been established. As long as the handler knows what commands the dog understands, the sounds required to control the animal's desperate wish to please, he or she will find a ready response.

Ask my wife! Shortly after Happy's whelping I went down with influenza necessitating ten days or so indoors, most of them in bed. On a one-man arable farm most jobs could be postponed; but naturally our housecows and pigs and calves and ducks and hens and of course sheep were not so obliging. The only answer was for my wife, supported as far as possible by the children, to step into the breach.

What she quickly discovered was that Happy worked just as well with her as with me, and as often as not appeared to recognize what was required, with little more than the initial command. When the sheep were being fed their supplementary winter concentrates, Happy unprompted was out of the tractor cab in a flash and keeping the hungry marauders away from the troughs even before my wife had heaved the bag from the trailer. And she continued to keep them at bay until my wife was well clear of the inevitable stampede.

I'm not saying that Happy wasn't sometimes caught in a conflict of loyalties. The first time I was able to get up and sit in a transplanted easy chair by the kitchen Rayburn, she looked bewildered and undecided as my wife called her to work the sheep. Should she go or stay with me? Desert me or follow my wife already disappearing through the kitchen door? Only the prospect of her favourite activity resolved the uncertainty.

My wife was intent upon putting the flock through a routine foot bath. I'd assured her it could wait, but she'd insisted there was no need. Wasn't she quite capable! So she was, curse the woman.

Actually she modestly claimed that Happy as good as did the job alone. For having been set in motion with the familiar *Away to me*, she knew what was required without further guidance, penning the flock, and pushing them nose to tail through the hock-deep antiseptic at a nice steady pace.

Meanwhile my wife, out of Happy's sight, was working the separating gate at the far end of the race, anxious to pick off three sheep whose wool, she said, looked tatty – large patches of bare skin showing. In fact, this proved to be nothing to worry about; but she wanted to reassure herself.

Less straightforward was what happened on the morning before I returned to work. This account is, of course, second-hand, and I can't hope to recapture my wife's eye-witness excitement; but knowing both the ram involved and Happy's lingering nipping lapses I can well imagine. Apparently the incident happened in three distinct stages.

Stage one. The younger ram was found roaming outside the meadow. Puzzle! No sign of any means of escape. The fences were sound, the barbed wire along the top intact. It was inconceivable he could have leaped over.

Stage two. Happy returned the ram to the meadow entrance with such speed my wife didn't have time to open the gate before he arrived, still pressed by the dog. Not now wanting to stay out, but not able to get in, he presumably panicked at Happy's persistence. The only way to escape the dog was to jump over her. He jumped. She jumped to stop his jump. They collided in mid air, and collapsed in a heap, the dog under the not inconsiderable weight of the frantic ram.

Stage three. Happy lost control, of herself as well as the ram. At least, that's what my wife reported. The offender bolted, pursued by the offended, and as quick as it was brief all hell was let loose. Happy found the ram's backside irresistible, and by all accounts wasn't entirely satisfied with mere nipping. She snapped and snarled, encouraging the ram, wanting nothing more than to go home, to give the opposite impression. The harder he ran, alas, in the wrong direction, the harder became Happy's counter attack. They were locked in a combat the ram didn't want and Happy couldn't win, not until that bloody gate was opened.

And to think this was the dog that a few short months before couldn't even walk!

With such incidents in mind, I wasn't surprised Bill Wheel's brother never tired of saying that a good flock needed a good shepherd as much as a good shepherd needed a good dog. Naturally it never occurred to me to disagree – until I watched sheepdog trials no more than three or four villages away. Actually, it wasn't so much the nearness that attracted me as the reputation of one of the entrants. He was due to run two dogs, both of them already winners, one reckoned to have enough promise to become a champion. And the mere fact that he thought it worth while to come more than two hundred miles suggested he expected this particular trials, never mind his dogs, to be rather special. I went, I can tell you, with high expectation.

The first three dogs to run were a disaster from beginning to end. The sheep were all over the place, missing gates by a mile, tearing off invariably in the wrong direction, utterly clueless, and finally scarpering off the course completely or creating maelstrom as they refused to be penned to complete the trials.

This wasn't all! Time after time the sheep positively defied the increasingly bewildered dogs, once or twice launching attacks. Never had I seen such obstinacy. Indeed, I began to wonder whether the sheep thought they were intended to do the herding. Seriously, it was almost as bad as that. All three handlers were retired for exceeding the time limit.

The quartettes of sheep were, I noticed, always the same selection of breeds – two Kents (Romneys), one black-face Suffolk, and one speckle-face cross breed of these two accurately called a mule, judging by the behaviour on this occasion.

These hybrids were unbelievably arrogant in the presence of the dogs, either themselves individually refusing to budge or taking the other three with them notably to frustrate both the shedding and final penning. None of this made sense, at least not to me.

The three breeds are part of our flock, and never especially difficult. Admittedly the mules did sometimes live up to their name, but what sheep doesn't! As I watched I concluded that either the dogs so far seen were out of their depth or the sheep – as sometimes happens inexplicably – were set on mischief.

Then I sat back to be impressed as the man with the first of his two outstanding dogs was called to the starting post. Proceedings were delayed a little as the handlers at the far end of the course tried to persuade the four sheep not to run back repeatedly for reunion with their buddies still waiting in the pen for use by later competitors. The men shouted, their dogs darted here and there trying to assist, but the sheep were single-minded. Come hell or high water they were not prepared for an easy parting.

Eventually they settled at the point of the lift, and the eager dog at the starting post was away. She made a beautiful outrun, closed in to make firm contact with the sheep, and was immediately confronted by a blank wall of bloody-mindedness.

The handler whistled like an old steamboat leaving port, the dog sharply responded like the potential champion she reputedly was, while the sheep, as though pulled by invisible chains, rushed only toward the pen. Never mind that the officials there shooed and booted, shouted and raged, the sheep remained obdurate, even when the two sheepdogs functioning from the pen mightily reinforced the futility of the competing dog which finally admitted defeat by watching the mayhem in astonished detachment.

After another five minutes or so the handler left the starting post to collect or rescue his dog, and departed the course muttering for all to hear that 'coming more than two hundred miles had been a bloody waste of time'.

Just so. These sheepdog trials were fast becoming a sick joke, a nightmare for the dogs no less than the buccaneering, but obviously in the main terrified, sheep. What in the world was going on? Fortunately, I recognized another competitor, a local farmer whose smile belied his frustration, though I must add he was remarkably philosophical about the total situation. The trouble is, he explained, these sheep are never worked by dogs; the silly buggers don't know what to do.

Ignoring for the moment how such a sizeable flock was managed without what in our experience was an absolute necessity, I asked whether it was usual for such untutored sheep to be used for sheepdog trials? After all, wasn't this something of a contradiction?

On the contrary, the local man insisted. Sheep farmers often had to work awkward sheep, accustomed to dogs or not. It was all part of the job. And in any case, he went on, at sheepdog trials what could be a better test – exactly the same for every competitor – than sheep at cross purposes with the dogs?

I saw his point, and immediately began a re-examination of the psychology of sheep. For a start, is their fear of the dog as I witnessed it daily on the farm instinctive or learned behaviour? No sooner had I asked myself the question than an image of Frank the sock lamb popped into my mind. She, you remember, preferred the company of two-legged sheep like the children who fussed her as much as they fussed Happy and Patch, frequently at the same time. The outcome was that Frank never really joined the flock, and therefore never reacted as they did notably in the presence of the dogs. The flock tended to scatter, at least to keep out of the way. Frank couldn't have cared less. If for whatever reason the dogs began to bark, the sheep were terrified; Frank on the other hand couldn't be bothered even to look up from grazing. Similarly, if the children were in the vicinity, dogs or no dogs, Frank hurled across. To be honest, I'm not positive she didn't think of herself as a dog, indistinguishable from our two who were more her playmates than anything else, allies not enemies.

Yet there's not the slightest doubt in my mind that if in the normal way she had been a member of the flock she would have reacted precisely as the rest did in the presence of a dog. A question of *learned* behaviour?

I'm aware that Frank was virtually humanized, and perhaps for that reason not a good test case, but her attitude to Happy and Patch surely raises this question of instinctive fear, if such it is. One thing remains beyond doubt. The handlers at the sheepdog trials, not least the man with his champion dogs, must have wished that the sheep's fear, whatever its origin, had been much more dominant.

There was, however, a delightful and in some ways inexplicable finale, incidentally still a talking point among sheepdog trials enthusiasts in our neighbourhood. It centred upon a retired shepherd whose only association with sheep these days is either as competitor or helper at sheepdog trials.

His flowing white beard makes him immediately distinctive in any company, but I call him to mind first of all as the wearer of old-fashioned steel-rimmed spectacles with tiny lenses through which he peers or searches rather than looks. How he sees anything at all, let alone distant sheep, is to me something of a mystery. Initially I met him at the very first trials I attended. He was responsible for penning the sheep after each run. A signal to his dog Pip, a casual stroll in step with his shepherd's crook, and the sheep meekly fell into line. Nothing to it. Of course, the sheep were tired, his vastly experienced dog was fresh each time, and the old shepherd himself had penned more sheep than a dozen average handlers between them. Nevertheless he made it look deceptively easy.

By any calculation he couldn't have been less than seventy though he (or rather his face) looked much older; *looked* as distinct from *behaved*, judging by his energy and – despite his rotundity – ramrod stance. Bill Wheel who knew him as well as anybody told me he lived alone, since his wife died unexpectedly soon after his retirement, and did everything for himself, refusing meals on wheels, and help with his washing and ironing from anybody including a married daughter. All welfare officials he viewed as nosyparkers, and vowed he'd die rather than accept charity.

I hadn't realized he was on this occasion a competitor until he and his faithful Pip took their place at the starting post, the pair of them by now typically having to wait while the quartette of sheep were marshalled. At last the old shepherd flicked his fingers, and the dog didn't hang about. Unlike the previous runners he approached from the left – though frankly I couldn't see that this provided any real advantage – and appeared sharply to cut in at the last moment to make a firm contact with the sheep, in normal circumstances perhaps too firm.

Anyhow, they shot off toward the first pair of gates, passed through the centre, and continued their co-operative way nicely round the shepherd's back, and on to the second gates. Then there was the first sign of trouble, initiated inevitably by the speckle-face mule. She faced the dog, the other three watching from the same position but not directly involved.

Concentrating exclusively on the leading sheep, Pip patrolled backwards and forwards three or four strides, actually turning his back as he retreated but always returning slightly nearer the sheep each time. In the end the two animals were almost touching, locked in uncompromising opposition. Suddenly the sheep went for the dog.

Whatever the judges thought of Pip's response I can only guess, but his fierce nipping and indeed biting were mightily effective. The mule saw red, blood from teeth marks on her nose, and massively capitulated. In a flash she was off, pursued by the other three, not to mention the dog, fortuitously in the direction of the gates, round the side with one sheep, the other two going through, all four to and straight through the centre of the third gates before veering round wide but still reasonably on course to the shedding ring, to be separated – as it proved with little help required from the dog – into any two pairs.

Ah, yes, but the speckle face wasn't done yet. At the penning, the shepherd shaking the rope attached to the gate, and waving his crook, Pip cagily approaching from the other side, she once more faced the dog for what transpired to be a repeat performance of the blood letting. The dog's tactics were precisely the same, unique in my experience – patrolling backwards and forward within three or four strides, inching nearer each time he again approached the sheep. They were so close finally that either the sheep had to back off or else! The result was another bloody nose, this time straight in front of the judges' position.

The old shepherd didn't win; wasn't even placed. But he and his dog at least convincingly made Bill Wheel's oft-repeated point that not all the best farm-working sheepdogs win the prizes at trials.

Another loser on an entirely different front unexpectedly arrived at the farmhouse some two months after Happy's whelping. My wife answered a knock at the kitchen door, called me, and there waiting shyly to greet me was the pale-maker from the woods. I hadn't seen him for ages. Over a cup of tea he told me of a recent frightening experience. Lost in his own private world as he maintained production under his battered tarpaulin, he was sharply brought back to self-awareness by an insistent noise getting closer. Over his shoulder he saw a four-legged juggernaut clearly resolved to ignore his determination to be friendly. Not a moment too soon, the laughing owner of the alsatian guard dog being exercised assured the woodman there was absolutely nothing to worry about. With me here, he added, he wouldn't do you any harm.

Still wondering what might have happened if the owner hadn't been handy, the woodman accepted from my wife a second cup of tea, one thing meanwhile remaining crystal clear. This normally ungregarious craftsman hadn't come only to chat about the playful guard dog. He looked uneasy, talked of this and that, with his mind clearly on something else. Did I know, he suddenly asked, that when a wolf, presumably the connection with his previous story, attacks a horse, it grabs the tail to pull the animal down? But if the horse in full flight is too strong, the wolf reinforces its attack by filling its stomach with soil, pounds and pounds of the stuff, and tries again. Mission this time successfully completed, it spews the earth out of its system, to enjoy the fruits of its ingenuity.

I admitted I didn't know about this, and thanked him for the enlightenment; but the feeling persisted that such a man who was more at home alone in the woods than making conversation in our farmhouse hadn't come simply to widen my knowledge of the wolf's hunting habits.

He glanced through the window, handed over his cup for another refill, told us about his need to get all his trees cut by the end of March, before the sap started to rise, and indulged in a little weather forecasting:

> If the oak is out before the ash,
> Then you'll only get a splash.
> But if the ash beats the oak,
> Then you can expect a soak.

These old country sayings, he concluded, are more trustworthy than the chaps on the radio. That's as maybe.

But he surely hadn't trekked to our back door to talk about the weather.

By the way, he nervously stirred as though to leave, I hear your bitch whelped? My wife filled in the details – seven superb puppies, sought by the whole world and his wife, all sold but one. His eyes lit up. The one, she responded smilingly, thinking he knew about Patch's replacement, the one we kept for ourselves.

Oh! his face dropped; I heard you had one left, he stammered, and hoped you'd let me have it. Then, as though screwing himself up, he stumbled over words in what sounded like a carefully rehearsed speech. Since seeing Happy with me in the woods, he'd often thought how nice it would be to have a dog. Like her. We'd seemed so contented together, real pals. And sometimes, though he didn't usually mind being on his own so much, he felt a bit lonely, no one to talk to for hours at a time. A dog like Happy would be perfect. And when he'd heard she'd whelped he'd wondered whether we'd be kind enough . . .

The words poured out. A cry from the heart.

Some weeks later Happy and I came across him in the woods. Came across *him*? First we spotted a black labrador puppy bounding toward us as friendly as could be, and soon I was hearing about a love affair at first sight.

Wasn't it, he laughed in unconscious irony, a good job you didn't let me have that whelp of yours? See what I would have missed! And looking at them together, I could not disagree.

I only wish the doves were so completely satisfied or satisfactory. The latest twist in their saga of surprises originated early one Saturday morning though they were at the time the least of my worries.

Long before first light the children were up, impatiently waiting for me to start the milking, let alone finish it; and immediately afterwards, no time for breakfast, the whole family including Happy jumped into the car, hoping we wouldn't after all be late.

Smoke from newly-lit cottage fires rose gently as we raced to the village green, rendezvous for any community spectacular. First to greet us was a man I'd often met also in the woods, a retired naval petty officer from the north inseparable on all occasions from his three whippets. They stood shivering in the lingering frost doubtless not a little bewildered as to why their customary lonely morning walk was suddenly proving irresistible to so many onlookers.

The whippet man, as we call him in the village, was talking to two officials, also whippet fans but on this occasion interested in nothing more than the weather. Periodically they scanned the sky, anxious, bemoaning the disaster of the previous week-end. 'That's why,' one of them despaired, 'we've only 3500 going this time.' He must have read the astonishment on my face. 'Nearer 17000 last time,' he explained; 'hundreds never found their way home.'

The pair of them commiserated with each other as to why racing pigeons, forced down by bad weather, appeared incapable of getting their bearings from the new take-off point. Even professors, people like that, they sounded incredulous, can't understand why.

Meanwhile the 3500 cooed their impatience to be off. They'd been brought in specially designed giant transporters the night before, a distance of nearly three hundred miles, and hopefully would be home long before the men from Durham and Yorkshire waiting to release them, men whose talk about their own pigeons was worthy of a lover wooing a reluctant mistress.

The cooing developed into a crescendo, suggesting the racers themselves realized the countdown was on. Officials, eyes glued on the chief marshal, waited for the signal to pull the synchronized levers that would open the front of the baskets. A whistle was blown. Ten seconds to go. Another blast, the levers clicked, and 3500 birds stormed into the air; a whirlwind of feathers tossed to and fro by nothing more than their own uncertainty about which way to go. They half circled the village green, turned back on themselves, seemed to hang in the air, then firmly headed north, bang on course, a stream of beating wings capable of sustaining speeds of fifty or so miles an hour for the estimated six-hour race.

Once the last of the stragglers was out of sight – and some, I must say, seemed reluctant to leave – the officials collected hatfuls of eggs from the baskets and shared them between the spectators. 'Lovely to eat,' one of them handed five to us. Then, not wasting a moment, they jumped into the three transporters, a whole day's hard drive ahead, their only reward the satisfaction of pigeon fanciers indulging their fanaticism.

'It's a way of life in the north,' one of them explained, 'a bloody way of life.' And with that they were away.

We too hurried home, and took down the frying pan. Pigeon eggs and bacon for breakfast! Only one oversight. We used the normal sized plates which somehow added to the loneliness of the eggs, but even so there was, we unanimously agreed, no doubting the pleasantness of their flavour.

Unfortunately, as you might have gathered, this wasn't the only memory left by the racing pigeons, one in particular. It liked our village so much it refused to leave, and eventually found its way to the dovecot in our front garden. After three or four days it gave up the unequal struggle to be given permanent roosting space, but not before mating with one of our promiscuous gang. How do we know? The fledglings were multi-coloured. I found them in the dovecot presumably pecked to death by the other doves.

We used to feel sorry for the doves because of the cats. Now we feel sorry for the doves because of the doves.

My wife felt sorry for the doves – two of them anyway – for a reason wholly unrelated to these murderous activities inside the dovecot. Driving with characteristic caution down our pitted farm track, she spotted a couple foraging directly in her path, slowed to a crawl but – assuming they'd have the sense to get out of the way – kept coming. Reaching the farmyard, barely bothering to check, she could hardly fail to see the corpses in her wake. And many times since we've both noticed how doves appear to imagine themselves impervious to danger from wheels of any kind.

But not to anything on four legs! Naturally they've adapted to living dangerously with the cats, and rarely these days give either our domesticated moggies or farm ferals any joy. Not that the cats stop trying; but the doves, idiots about wheels, check the vicinity with a visual toothcomb before descending for the daily feed.

In the early days, as I've mentioned, the fledglings stood little chance of surviving their first couple of days out of the dovecot unless protected by human vigilance, yet their recent counterparts have somehow picked up the message and now never leave the dovecot until capable of flying directly on to the farmhouse roof. Ain't nature wonderful!

And sometimes unnatural. Bill Wheel turned up one day to tell me he'd just seen a rabbit chasing a stoat. Chasing? Well, said Bill, it was *following* the stoat, to all intents and purposes chasing; and this led him to reminisce about the times he'd watched a fox, clearly seeing a rabbit within killing distance, appear contented to give the quarry living space.

What's more, how come a stinking fox and a badger as clean as a new pin share part of the same earth? Don't make sense, he summed up.

Occasionally I thought this about Happy's senseless attitude to the sheep. For weeks she wouldn't show the slightest inclination to nip, let alone bite, then one perfectly ordinary day she'd go berserk. I never really understood why. I wasn't averse to a few teeth marks in the right quarter – but always at the back of my mind was the distinction between a dog working sheep and winning trials. For I still hankered after proving that Happy was better than merely a first-class farm dog, in spite of the fact that Bill and a few farmers like him continued to argue a good working dog had nothing to prove.

Probably I would have done nothing had another series of One Man And His Dog not started. Don't misunderstand me. It wasn't that I thought Happy was in the same class, well, not all the time, but one of the dogs featured so resembled my dog in appearance and to a degree that I found myself seriously wondering just how good she was.

The morning after one programme I took her to our miniature course in the meadow, and watched spellbound as she demonstrated not only her basic skills, but initiative in nipping NOT backsides but impending trouble in the bud. Sheer magic. Surely a dog of this ability was worthy of novice sheepdog trials! Surely.

Surprisingly my wife disagreed. She quietly insisted that after Happy's accident and the death of Patch she didn't, as she put it, want to tempt Providence by stepping outside essential and thoroughly understood routine. If Happy managed the sheep on the farm, and kept out of trouble, what more could we ask? Trials or no trials, she was a marvellous sheepdog. Let's leave it at that.

Hearing her talk, like a recording of Bill Wheel on the warpath, I began to wonder whether my nagging wish to enter Happy was in effect an insult to the dog, a demand that she prove what was already self-evident almost every day on the farm. She was deeply involved in another lambing season, separating singles and twins and triplets with ever growing confidence, helping to persuade bereaved ewes to adopt hungry orphans, keeping the rams firmly in their place, stopping the stampede as nutty concentrates were daily poured into the troughs, and generally facilitating an easier life for the shepherd and his hard-pressed wife. She was absolutely right. What more could we ask?

And doubtless that would have remained our united conclusion, but for another handwritten note from the secretary of our county sheepdog society. It arrived on April 11th. The date is important, as I shall explain in a moment, and I can be so precise because that morning I heard my first cuckoo of the year.

The handwritten note brought to my attention that novice sheepdog trials were to be held on Saturday week – ten days away – and further that I still wasn't too late to be included. As though this wasn't enough, the good man was generous in his remembrance of Happy's perform-ance at the nursery trials. I was both amazed and moved.

217

To be remembered at all was incredible; that he should go the extra mile and actually take the trouble to write was irresistible. My entry form was forwarded by return of post.

Having committed myself the reaction was, I suppose, inevitable. The blood coursed through my veins, pumped round by apprehension, excitement, the extremes of confidence and despair – and simple panic. At the same time the pressure of ten short days concentrated the mind wonderfully, and also brought a new urgency into all my working relationships with Happy. Whether she was aware of this quickened tempo is an open question, but there's little doubt in my mind she picked up that something special was on.

At every opportunity I put her through her paces, grabbing fifteen or twenty minutes here and there sometimes unnecessarily to work the sheep. Nothing ambitious. Just a few exercises in basic skills, almost welcoming the awkwardness of the occasional ewe or ewes to test Happy's responses.

And straightaway I transferred the practice course to our biggest field, twice the size of our average, with a couple of testing obstacles – a pond of some depth at one end, and a hollow usually containing water at the other. As soon as I could get away from routine chores for half an hour or more, usually between lunch and afternoon milking, Happy and I set to work with five ewes deliberately chosen for their lack of ready co-operation.

From the pond end of the field I could barely see the point where Happy contacted the sheep at the other, also the boundary of the wood. In other words, until she brought them some distance on the fetch, she was working beyond the reach, certainly the easy reach, of my voice. Occasionally she lacked confidence, looking back for reassurance or guidance, maybe both, but not once did she fail to reach the sheep nicely behind them or set them firmly on their way.

I wonder, though, why it is that when things are going so well, notably on a farm like ours, the unexpected seems incapable of keeping its nose clean!

It was Sunday morning, six days before the trials. Happy and I were making our way to the practice course when suddenly in the distance I saw a man rush out of the wood, and not hesitating for a moment wade fully dressed into the hollow of water. He splashed and kicked around, apparently struggling with something. I started to run, and soon realized he was holding a lamb, cradling it like a baby. Seeing us approaching, he too started to run, in our direction, shouting unintelligibly. Desperately he handed me the lamb which admittedly looked more dead than alive, but was soon restored and anxious to be re-united with its mum in the adjacent field, apparently none the worse for its near drowning.

The rescuer explained he'd been on the public pathway through the wood when he'd spotted the drama, obviously in the nick of time. I thanked him, of course, and wondered aloud about his trousers saturated with stagnant water hardly noted for its fragrance. Brushing this little inconvenience aside as though it happened every day, he casually suggested that, if I didn't mind, he'd wring them out forthwith, and continue his walk; in this lovely weather they'd soon dry out.

Since coming here we'd had a few comic scenes, but never a man in his underpants wringing out polluted trousers in the middle of a field. Discreetly I enquired whether the farmhouse might be more suitable; and finally, as he started the unbuttoning, had almost to drag him to seclusion, so anxious was he not to make a nuisance of himself!

At the farmhouse he sat entwined in my dressing gown while I scraped off the worst of the scum at the cowshed tap, and made a similar gesture at the kitchen sink. Then with the slightly less pungent garment out of the spin drier and steaming foul incense in front of the Rayburn, we settled down to drink coffee and talk. And talk.

Our unexpected guest turned out to be a walking chapter of unfortunate coincidences, the most optimistic pessimist I'd ever met or am likely to meet. His whole philosophy was cheerfully based on the assumption or expectation – based congenitally, he claimed – that things were bound to go wrong or at least not right. Like this morning! He didn't, he emphasized, go *looking* for trouble; it just happened, far more often than not. But there *were* compensations! If he hadn't finished up in our pond, as he called it, he wouldn't be sitting drinking coffee in a seventeenth-century farmhouse.

'I'd rather face trouble any day,' he laughed, 'than uneventful routine. Wouldn't you?' his eyes passed between my wife and me.

'Not really,' she spoke for us both.

By now his trousers were bone dry, but unmindful of both his walk and our appointment on the trials course, we were lost in fast and furious conversation. This colourful character who seemed to meet setbacks at every turn held us spellbound, not to say amused, with some of his reminiscences. Amused? He was that kind of man, relating one disaster after another, and roaring with laughter at his unbelievable ineptitude. But the stories weren't all funny, the very opposite. He told us, for instance, of his father dying on Christmas Eve, of his wife two days later going into hospital for a serious operation, and of himself visiting her, getting his foot entangled in a seat belt as he stepped out of the car, and breaking his ankle.

Yes, but did these 'coincidences', we asked, all of them fortuitous and open to happen to anyone, indicate or even induce an attitude of mind that unconsciously attracted misfortune? He thought there might be something in this, but reiterated that people with a tendency to pessimism were born not made.

All this time Happy who normally kept well clear of all strangers was snugly settled at his feet, utterly confident. Periodically he bent to knead her ears, picture of a man who loved and understood dogs. Yet he didn't own one himself, though if he did, he explained, it would be a sheepdog. Do you by any chance watch One Man And His Dog? he asked.

Happy and I eventually walked him back to the wood, he and I shook hands, and he disappeared among the trees, presumably wondering what next would go wrong or at least not quite right. A strange but stimulating man, almost a phantom, for we haven't seen or heard of him since. The only piece of evidence he left that he wasn't a figment of our imagination was, of course, the lamb which became one of our best.

That afternoon we at least managed an hour's training and as we strolled satisfied back to the cowshed I couldn't fail to notice the cutter parked behind the Tyler barn, forceful reminder of that terrible accident. Instinctively I looked down at Happy's feet firmly treading the grass and farmyard concrete, not a suspicion of discomfort or restriction. Some recovery! Now here we were on the threshold of our second sheepdog trials!

The next day's training, this time in the early evening, was again restricted by a family appointment in the village hall, unthinkable to miss, one to which the entire village had looked forward with a mixture of pleasure and regret. Our village postman was retiring after thirty-two years of courteous service.

As comparative newcomers we knew Walter only as grey haired and slightly bent backed, but many villagers remembered his arrival shortly after the war and his unbroken deliveries since. Now I recognize how difficult it must be for outsiders to appreciate the bond that can develop between a village and, say, its postman or policeman or milkman or post office factotum. These usually anonymous characters in the city take on distinctive identities in small, compact communities; and Walter was an outstanding case in point.

Paradoxically, this gentle man was the only person I knew who ever really terrified Happy, just the once; as much my fault as his. He'd been having a spot of bother with dogs, not the harmless yapping type but the occasional man eaters who compelled him to run the gauntlet if his duties were to be fulfilled. Not that Walter was easily intimidated. He was countryman enough to know that dogs are tamed by nothing more than a fearless approach. Put contrariwise, that they smell fear in humans, fear which provokes them instinctively to assert their pack authority.

Nonetheless, Walter wasn't stupid, given to going out of his way to tempt fate. So when his wife anxiously demanded he get for himself a protection alarm, notwithstanding his initial merriment at the idea, he accepted one as a gift. From her. And was soon able gratefully to assure her it worked like magic. It was, to be precise, as he told me too of this latest escapade with a giant guard dog that unconsciously we colluded in Happy's eventual discomfiture: Walter's offer to demonstrate the tiny instrument in his pocket was as unthinking in the circumstances as my immediate acceptance.

Happy herself knew Walter as well as anybody outside the farm, and unhesitatingly wagged her tail in welcome each time he cycled to our door. On this occasion she received his customary kindly words and pats, as unsuspecting as any trusting dog could be. Laughingly he switched the protection alarm on. I heard nothing. But Happy took off howling and disappeared like a scalded cat into the cowshed, obviously terrified. The reason, Walter explained, was a noise or signal of some sort too high for human hearing but fearfully audible to the dog.

Still laughing he climbed on his bike, while I, no less sharing his amusement, I admit, went in search of Happy to offer needed assurance and fussing. She obviously forgave us both, for I was granted her usual enthusiastic companionship, and Walter continued to receive his tail-wagging welcome.

The arrangements in the village hall for his retirement were no less ungrudging. The chairman of the parish council expressed inadequate thanks on behalf of us all, and presented a lawn mower purchased by public subscription, before Walter briefly responded. He was, he said, an ordinary postman by deliberate choice. Let others climb the institutional career ladder; all he had ever wanted was to continue to deliver letters in our village. He'd seen children born, start school, go out to work, get married and have children of their own; he'd watched many villagers retire, enjoy the fruits of a hard-working life, grow old graciously, and finally quietly slip away, mourned by a whole community; he'd been a confidant and confessor, sharer of the village's joys and sorrows, privileged to call so many of his appreciative customers his personal friends. What more, he concluded, could any man ask?

To thunderous applause he and his wife stood side by side while the entire village, or so it seemed, already caught up in a festive mood, queued to wish personally a long happy retirement. Then the dancing started.

Have you ever been to a barn dance? Young and old unself-consciously throw themselves about without regard to barriers of age, sex or dancing skill. No one is excluded, even those who – for reasons of physical or temperamental disability – prefer to watch on the sidelines. I tell you it incorporates *everybody*. And if this sounds unreal, I don't argue or apologize; simply insist the half hasn't been told.

I saw Walter talking with a man twenty years his senior, one with a near life-time behind him of delivering lambs, the other of delivering letters. Old Dick placed his horny hand on the postman's shoulder, and their weather beaten faces shone with rare contentment. My wife followed my eyes, and – not given to religious utterances – whispered: Blessed are the meek, for they shall inherit the earth. In spite of my less than serious reaction I think I understood what she was getting at. In any case, I laughed only because I was reminded of the one occasion in my experience when Walter brought his usually discreet sagacity loudly to bear upon one of the rich farmers in the district. He was, the village postman summed him up, so sure the meek inherited the earth he tried to bully everybody else into accepting the same point of view.

The festivities were in full swing when reluctantly our family withdrew, not because it was already long past the children's bedtime, but the prospect of my getting up at first light to do the milking was losing its appeal by the minute. I crawled into bed, and fell asleep thinking of the sheepdog trials five days ahead.

Tuesday. Happy and I didn't have a chance to work the course, though as things turned out it made little difference to her involvement with the sheep. We rotated their pasture, and also spent quite a bit of time picking off four lambs and their mums for closer inspection. The lambs appeared not to be doing as well as the others, and I wanted to be sure the ewes had plenty of milk. In the event, the only trouble was with one ewe which had an extended udder on one side through her lamb insisting upon suckling exclusively on the opposite teat.

We'd come across this once before, and knew therefore that the only answer was hand milking the ignored teat. In itself this presented something of a problem, for to take off milk, whatever the method, was naturally to trigger its replenishment, the very thing I wanted to avoid. My aim was simply to reduce pressure on the disused side of the udder without hindering its drying off as quickly as possible. There was, I knew, more than enough nourishment for the lamb from the one teat.

I imagine a lamb's occasional allergy to a teat, left or right, is comparable to Happy's distinct preference for a left-handed approach on the gather. The difference is that nothing on earth seems capable of persuading the lamb spontaneously to feed from the rejected teat. Why, I've no idea. The only thing I'm sure about is the amount of extra work involved until the untapped side of the udder adjusts. The discomfort for the ewe can be imagined; rather like a human mother with one breast as tight as a drum while her child feeds incorrigibly on the other. It doesn't happen, of course, but you see the problem for the poor old sheep when she faces such a situation.

The other diversion as I frantically tried to find time to get Happy on the trials course was a minor breakout of the sheep, minor in the sense we spotted it almost as it happened, but the exact opposite when it came to repairing the fence. I set out intending to do a makeshift job until after the trials, but soon realized that even this involved major labour; far better, all things considered, to do the job properly. When it was finished three or so hours later, though absolutely delighted with the fence, I was far enough behind with routine chores to eliminate any possibility of practice on the course.

Wednesday was no better. One of those days, in fact, when I never seemed to stop yet at the end of it all wondered where in the world the time had gone – one job after another, each of them essential but adding up to little more than frustration and no trials course. Ah, well, tomorrow was another day.

Happy and I were actually on our way to the course before the children left for school the next morning. Let the sky fall, I was resolved to fit in at least one training session during the day, the earlier the less likely of cancellation. I saw them climb into the car and heard the engine turning over lifelessly. My wife called. I lifted the bonnet, fiddled with a few wires, cleaned the plugs, checked the points; and accepted defeat. Everybody out.

The children loved going to school in the trailer anyway, but my wife drew the line at driving on public highways. So Happy jumped into her customary place in the cab, and we were off, my irritation counterbalanced by the children's noisy excitement. The tractor and empty trailer were back by just after nine o'clock. Parked in the farmyard was a blue van out of which the driver characteristically unwound himself.

Bill's unexpected visits, though sparse, were not altogether either unusual or surprising. He invariably pitched up unannounced, for a definite purpose unrelated to passing the time of day, but always between lunch and afternoon milking. At this hour he should have been up to his ears in work that couldn't wait. Problem was, he hurriedly explained, his young driver had half slipped the tractor into a ditch. Could I take ours to pull it out? Shouldn't take more than twenty minutes at most.

At one o'clock I returned to the farmyard to find my wife wondering when I would be free for lunch? And then the jobs I'd postponed from the morning to accommodate my determination to spend time on the trials course awaited urgent attention, plus all the normal afternoon jobs! Happy and I seemed fated.

Even before we started the following morning, Friday, I knew things would be little different. Half-a-dozen lambs had to be picked off and delivered to the abattoir. True, Happy was deeply involved, but in nothing like the challenge of a fetch and drive and shedding and penning to trials standard. Beyond argument she did what was required with competence, certainly to my convenience and satisfaction, but whether fastidious judges would share my assessment was another matter.

We did manage a brief session on the course before afternoon milking, and another after supper, but neither was of the stuff of which eve-of-trials confidence is made. Happy was a bit of everything – brilliant, diabolical, sharp, sluggish, firm, fierce, steady, impetuous. One moment I was inwardly cheering, certain I was on to a winner, the next groaning at her unbelievable cluelessness.

It was, I suppose, the old old story – my apprehension communicating itself to the dog. We remained on the course until near dark, trying the fetch again. And again. Encouraging Happy to bring the sheep tighter round my back for the drive. Tighter! She would persist in pushing them too wide, perfectly acceptable on a farm, but on the morrow! And how many times did we attempt the shedding and penning! Far far too many, judging by the way her inconsistency added to my uncertainty. Or should that be the other way round? Whatever the answer, I at least returned to the farmhouse convinced we were destined for ignominy.

The alarm the next morning sounded like the music of hell. Screwed up after a tossing and turning sort of night I staggered out of bed and groped my way to the kitchen. Happy characteristically was on her toes, tail wagging, eyes full of welcome, impatient to start what she supposed was another ordinary day.

I sipped coffee, felt life slowly returning, and set off for the cowshed, Happy initially tearing about the field to celebrate the freedom of the morning, before walking uncommanded to heel.

Self-consciously trying to play it cool, I commenced the milking, fed the lurking ferals the usual first half pint, and settled to finish the job as quickly as possible. Radio Two blared in the background, hard for me to take at this unearthly hour, but apparently appreciated by the animals. No joking. One day I happened to switch it on during milking, and the cow inclined to kick immediately steadied, not a sign of trouble since. Might have been merely a coincidence, but I'd no wish to push my luck. Music while you milk was for us a must!

I rested my head against the former kicker's sweet smelling, warm and snug belly, and was further soothed by the rhythmic sound of squirts into the bucket between my legs; soporific, pleasing inducement to relaxation. Our new young cockerel belatedly heralded the dawn. Happy herself was in and out, anxious to miss nothing in either cowshed or farmyard. I heard the hens squawk, not chased by the dog, I was sure, but doubtless taken unawares simply by her approach as they foraged near the entrance to the ancient barn, favourite place for daily renewed pickings.

The ferals, stuffed beyond capacity, purred near my feet; untamable aristocrats, drugged by satiation, blissfully content.

My feelings, I admit, were less unmixed – tranquil but uptight. The adrenalin was flooding. Deep within myself I was utterly (and I must say happily) abandoned to the disasters of the day.

With a coiled spring in our steps, Happy and I returned to the farmhouse to find the usual breakfast scrummage already well underway. The children, notably the younger two, were irrepressible, caught up in their primary concern which was unashamedly unrelated to the sheepdog trials. Happy might be their favourite sheepdog – excluding, maybe, the new puppy – and their noisy certainty she was going to win remained unshaken; but one of the numerous innovations on the day's programme commanded their exclusive interest.

The pet lamb competition!

Actually, I'm embarrassed even to mention it in juxtaposition to the real issues of what lay ahead, but its disproportionate influence on the family's attitude to the trials can neither be overlooked nor entirely forgiven. The organizers of sheepdog trials need, I appreciate, to widen public appeal, but in our farmhouse that wretched pet lamb competition dominated everything, from such weighty deliberations about which two lambs to enter, to how best and at what point to finalize their toiletry preparations.

By the time the car was loaded and we all climbed in, the chosen two, already smelling like a beauty salon, were causing more fuss than all other considerations put together, Happy included. It was almost indecent. An indignity to the dog, never mind the lambs. From now on I shall try, in the name of sanity, not to mention the matter again.

The trials were due to begin at 10.30 A.M.. We arrived about an hour before, to be signalled by an unnervingly polite policeman to a car park reserved for dog handlers only, the first of our surprises.

Surprise number two was the early carnival atmosphere, not unlike the nursery novice trials but altogether more festive, like a public holiday at its best. Clearly we expected trade stands, an exhibition of sheep shearing and country crafts generally, a wool display, and the clay pigeon shoot, all of them prominent on the programme; but preeminent in terms of both size and appeal was a children's fairground, and, coming a close second in popularity, a display of flying model aircraft. Somehow it never crossed my mind that a Wellington bomber and Messerschmitt fighter might be swooping around as Happy and I set about trying to impress the judges!

Surprise number three, not so unexpected but in the event absolutely breathtaking, was the scenic setting of the trials course – gentle rolling downs as far as the eye could see, brought into sharper focus by spring sunshine and a cloudless blue sky. Simply stunning.

The children disappeared to find the marquee, centre of their obsession for the day, while all competing sheepdog handlers were asked to report at a huge Land Rover, later called into service as the judges' grandstand. Strolling across with Happy on a lead, I hoped to renew acquaintances from the nursery novice trials, but every face was new, some of them, I soon discovered, belonging to handlers of vast experience. And it was among this group, not all of them professional shepherds, that a heated argument developed.

It centred upon a car and its driver, the car a Volvo made conspicuous by the name emblazoned on its sides of a well-known brand of cigarette, with alongside in smaller but still distinctive letters the name and function of the driver, a sheepdog trials competitor. His sponsorship, the first of its kind I'd come across or even heard about, was evidently not universally popular!

One handler in particular, a farmer, passionately argued that sponsorship was bringing hard professionalism into what was meant to be nothing more than a sporting pastime, a trend, he said, guaranteed to destroy a lot of fun, discourage beginners from competing, and finally make money a greater concern than the trialing itself.

The contrary point of view was presented with equal vehemence, the result being that long before the first partnership went to the starting post an initially friendly verbal punch-up was turning decidedly nasty. Perhaps it says something about human nature that the semblance of harmony was only restored after the sponsored handler and his dog, named, incidentally, after the brand of cigarette, were retired by the judges for exceeding the time limit, retired after a disastrous run from the first moment. Money no doubt talks; but apparently not loud enough always to win sheepdog trials.

To be fair, I picked up early in the day that the solitary sponsored handler wasn't expecting to win. The dog he was running, though full of promise, was young and very inexperienced, even at our modest level. Not that the course facing us was a walkover, far from it, but at least its demands were thought to be within the ability of nursery novice and novice sheepdogs. By the way, after two wins in this class a dog moved into the open novice class, again until registering two wins, after which open championships were the goal.

For the moment Happy and I were content in the nursery novice class, though on this occasion the trials were classified as novice. This didn't mean we were thinking above ourselves; nursery and novice sheepdogs usually, in fact, compete against each other. Very few sheepdog societies even bother to make the distinction.

Following the sponsored partnership, the dog next on the programme, never a winner in a separate nursery class, was already one win down and one to go as a novice. His age, given as two years, took a bit of believing; he looked comprehensively mature as literally he strained at the leash. For Ben was tied to the front bumper of his handler's car parked opposite the shedding ring, the pair of them keenly watching each competitor, and every time a dog with the sheep passed this vantage point Ben went berserk, wildly impatient to lend assistance. Consequently, or so it seemed to me, by the time he and his handler were called to the starting point, the dog at least was too excitable to be either in control of himself or strictly within his handler's.

Nevertheless, they started well enough, Ben's gather being beautifully pear shaped, with the lift as firm as a rock, too firm, in fact. The sheep were startled and set off on the fetch in something of a panic, fortunately shooting through the first set of gates dead centre, but thereafter too agitated to appease Ben's growing impetuosity.

His undoubted class was glimpsed in the shedding ring where the sheep, now thoroughly disturbed, jostled around, never still for a moment, making it extremely difficult for the handler to find a gap between the sheep wearing a red collar and the rest to call in his dog. When he did, eventually, the shedding was completed only by Ben's split-second response.

More impressive generally was the next partnership, a farmer's wife and five-year-old Cap, running in his first trials. His gather, if as good, was certainly no better than Ben's, but his first contact with the sheep, well-nigh perfect, gave him an immediate advantage. They trotted toward the first set of gates, almost strolled through the centre, and with little apparent prompting from the dog turned tight behind the handler to begin the drive.

Cap's eyes never once left the sheep, and his response to every whistled command was virtually instantaneous. Indeed, few commands appeared necessary. The sheep passed through the second gates, for instance, and were immediately turned by the dog alone toward the next set of gates. True, this remarkable standard wasn't maintained throughout, notably as the sheep approached the shedding ring. One of them inexplicably shot off to the right, and became increasingly bolshie as the dog wasted no time in seeking to regain control. Only Cap's no-nonsense attitude, as determined a piece of herding, short of nipping, as any harassed shepherd could wish to see, prevented a potentially chaotic development. Even so, a degree of confusion wasn't altogether resolved at either the shedding or penning, though both remained mightily impressive.

Chatting to his handler soon afterwards I gathered she was normally too busy with her large goat herd to bother with sheep at all, let alone sheepdog trialing. Her husband was the shepherd of the family. Then why was she and not he running the dog? Because, she shyly explained, Cap, apart from working the sheep with her husband, also helped her with the goats.

It was impossible to hide my disbelief. In my experience goats were difficult enough to handle by humans, never mind a sheepdog. Surely they would simply put their heads down and charge. Laughingly she admitted this was sometimes the case, but still insisted that Cap, though frequently challenged and defied, was able to assert enough authority to make goat herding easier. I suspect she was being much too modest when she added that her love affair with the goats made their control no trouble at all.

What was patently obvious was the contribution the goats had made to Cap's working of the sheep, for he exhibited a quality of strength and determination, no hesitation, no messing, that was bound to quieten the toughest of ewes simply by making them unmistakably aware of what was required.

By the break for lunch I had no doubt that Cap was the dog to beat. What the judges thought was, of course, something else, but I reckoned that his penalty points couldn't have been more than fifteen from a maximum score of a hundred, astronomic and, I feared, beyond Happy even at her best.

Reminding myself sheepdog trials, particularly at our level, were meant to be fun, a day out for the family, I set off with Happy to find my wife and children whose

234

interest in the trials themselves beyond Happy's participation had long surrendered to other attractions. Naturally they wanted to see Happy's run, but as we were the penultimate partnership on the programme sadly it looked as though their preoccupation with the pet lamb competition would make this impossible.

We ate our sandwiches and emptied the coffee flasks. I looked at my watch. Still thirty-five minutes to go before the trials recommenced! My wife suggested I should take the opportunity to buy a pair of handmade farm boots, the work of a young craftsman within a family business established by his grandfather, a name with an enviable reputation. But I was too keyed up to do anything but aimlessly walk about and try to share some of the children's excitement about their pet lambs.

We watched a shearer remove a complete fleece, one piece, in a minute and a half; a weaver looking more like a city gent than a country craftsman; a lace maker throwing her bobbins from hand to hand with the speed of a circus juggler; a couple of working steam engines proving that craftsmanship at the beginning of the century was nothing if not a guarantee of longevity for everything produced; and chatted, my wife and I, with officials at a stand featuring a trust formed to protect endangered and rare breeds of British livestock. Yet still the minutes dragged, one by reluctant one bringing me nearer to what I dreaded but longed to get behind me.

As Happy and I, myself thoroughly screwed up, strolled back to the course, I decided that this time we wouldn't watch, but would simply stand back quietly on our own, and wait to be called.

Two hours later, weary of hanging about, past caring, we stood together at the starting post, Happy on her toes, impatient to be off, I staring into the distance as the five sheep were ushered into position. They settled, and I received the signal.

Come bye, I whispered. My heart raced as Happy made her approach rather too tight but not enough to startle the sheep. The lift was firm. Excellent. The sheep unhurriedly moved toward the first gates, passed through to the right, and continued bang in line with me to complete the fetch. Suddenly I felt exhilarated, relaxed. This really was *fun*! It seemed as though, in a way I'd rarely if ever experienced before, that Happy and I were somehow plugged into the same wavelength. I remember feeling indescribably happy, proud, carefree. The nearest spectators must have wondered as I laughed out loud for no apparent reason.

Happy, eyes riveted, crouched low, beautifully keeping her distance, brought on the five, moved to her left to shove them behind me, and started the drive, not a suggestion of trouble. *Steady*, I called as she pushed the sheep through the next gates, and anticipated my *Come bye* to turn them for the cross drive and the third set of gates some two hundred strides away.

Proverbially every dog has its day; and this, no doubt, was Happy's. She was performing far above herself, too utterly wrapped up in the job in hand to care about trials judges or spectators or model aeroplanes or even the still over-zealous sheepdog tied to the car bumper too near the boundary of the course! As I viewed my dog calmly pushing on those oh so co-operative sheep, I began to calculate.

Eighteen out of twenty for the gather, ten out of ten for the lift, surely twenty out of twenty for the fetch, and just as surely not a mark dropped so far on the drive. It was uncanny. I couldn't believe the undeniable. The sheep tamely trotted through the third set of gates, and headed for me at the shedding ring.

Inexplicably they veered a little to their left, countered almost immediately by Happy, but not soon enough to keep them entirely beyond the influence of the dog tied to the bumper. Ben appeared to go mad, tearing at the leash, barking like crazy, and stopping only to renew his frantic efforts to break free.

The leading sheep bolted, taking two with her, ninety degrees to the right heading straight back to the penning area behind the point of the lift. For a moment I was transfixed, flummoxed. Presumably on the farm, less enraptured, I would have leapt into action, working immediately with the dog to restore order. On this occasion the magic of the previous minutes had apparently lulled my reflexes into some sort of paralysis. My mouth fell open, and for a fatal delay I was dumbstruck.

Not that this inhibited Happy. In a flash she gave chase of the two sheep going hell for leather toward the second set of gates. Meanwhile Ben kept barking as though possessed by demons; barking and tearing at the leash until I thought he might be in danger of breaking his neck.

Eventually, with a little judicious nipping to hasten proceedings, some sort of order was restored, and we completed the shedding and penning within the time limit; just. I can't swear the nipping influenced the judges in the final result, but beyond question the winning dog, in my humble opinion, wasn't even placed.

And here's another funny thing. I appeared to be the only one who seriously believed the scattering of the sheep had absolutely nothing to do with Happy. Sheepdogs, it was again pointed out, were expected to cope with any contingency, a rogue dog of whatever sort included. In any case, the dog near the boundary of the course was tied up! What more could any responsible owner be expected to do?

To add insult to injury, the pet lamb competition was also a disaster. One of our lambs won.

Back on the farm in time for a belated afternoon milking the two over-loaded housecows mooed their protest at being kept waiting. Once more I snuggled my head against the former kicker's soft warm belly, rhythmically pulling her teats, while she contentedly munched her ration of cow cake; once more the ferals indulged themselves with the first half pint as Happy repeated her comings and goings between cowshed and farmyard, to the accompaniment of the hens re-echoing their squawking at her innocent approach – the whole scene such a re-enactment of the dawn milking that the intermission might never have happened at all.

Perhaps it never did – at least, not as I shall always remember it, a superb working sheepdog robbed of victory by a yapping trialist of reputedly greater promise. But what does it matter, finally?

As wearily we walked back to the farmhouse, Happy faithfully to heel, wide awake, ready if need be to work her heart out as the other side of our partnership, I bent to knead her ears, and tell her what I at least could never doubt again.

She was a winner!